NEWTONMORE

SIGNAL BOX

BOOK REF: _____O6l___

WALKING
WEST COUNTRY
RAILWAYS

Christopher Somerville

DAVID & CHARLES
Newton Abbot London North Pomfret (Vt)

FOR NIGEL WILLIS AND THE RAILWAY RAMBLERS

The Author wishes to emphasise that walkers should gain permission from the owner before entering any disused railway land.

British Library Cataloguing in Publication Data

Somerville, Christopher
　Walking West Country railways.
　1. Railroads – South-west England – Abandonment – History 2. South-west England – Description and travel – Guidebooks
　I. Title
　385'.09423　　　　　HE3019.S
　ISBN 0–7153–8143–1

Typeset by Northern Phototypesetting Co., Bolton and printed in Great Britain by A. Wheaton & Co. Ltd., Hennock Road, Exeter for David & Charles (Publishers) Limited Brunel House, Newton Abbot, Devon

Published in the United States of America by David & Charles Inc. North Pomfret, Vermont 05053, USA

CONTENTS

INTRODUCTION –
THE WEST COUNTRY

The West Country! Surfing beaches and granite rocks of Cornwall, rich red earth and clotted cream of Devonshire, a herd of cows lazily heading for home in a narrow Somerset lane, the chalk Downs of the Dorset coast lands; these, with the throaty burr of the local speech and the sharp tang of scrumpy cider, sand in the sandwiches and fishing boats by the jetty, call up the flavour of sunny holidays in the green toe of England. For all the generations since the railways first opened up the south-west corner of the country to outsiders, the West Country has stood for unchanging values, for an unaffected friendliness among the inhabitants, for largely unspoilt countryside where those weary of the concrete wilderness can refresh body and spirit among scenes revisited infrequently but treasured in retrospect all year long.

But where exactly *is* the West Country? Bristol is the gateway to the West – so the Bristolians say. Along the line of the Brendon Hills and the Exe Valley lies the border of the West Country – or such is the boast of Tiverton and Exeter. To reach the proper heart of the West you must penetrate the hearts of Exmoor and Dartmoor, according to people who live in those two great National Parks; while for any self-respecting Cornishman the River Tamar marks the boundary between the real West Countryman and the outlandish inhabitants of the rest of the world.

This book is about the delights and frustrations of walking the abandoned railways of the West Country. I have chosen the track of one of Dr Beeching's victims to serve as the boundary to the West – the Somerset & Dorset Railway, a virtual coast to coast barrier that runs for 71½ miles from Bath in the north to Bournemouth in the south. West of the grassy embankments and overgrown cuttings of the S&D lies the territory covered in these pages.

This irregular triangle of land embraces the Mendip Hills and the flat plains of the Somerset levels, the Dorset Downs and

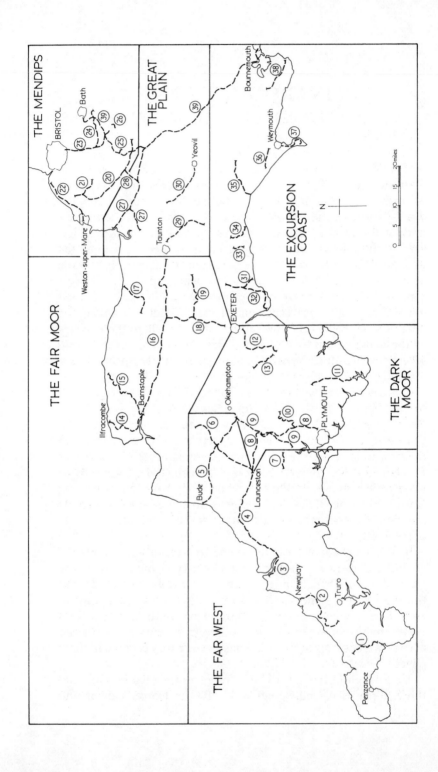

holiday resorts, the Brendon and Quantock hills, Exmoor, Dartmoor, and Bodmin Moor, all the peaceful rural uplands and valleys of Devon and the whole of the Cornish kingdom. To all the points of the compass across this huge slice of Britain run the tracks of the disused railways. Some linked a handful of tiny villages along a few miles of river valley or moorland, shoestring concerns that were born unheralded and died unnoticed; others were major through routes which carried passengers in their hundreds of thousands every year to the substantial towns and cities of the West Country – Bournemouth, Exeter, Plymouth, Launceston, Barnstaple and many more. All had their devotees, attracted by the beauties of the countryside and the distinctive flavour of the towns served by the railways, or by the idiosyncracies of the stationmasters, porters, signalmen and drivers that made each line different from its neighbour, or by the chuffing tank engines and thundering expresses. All were reduced to silence and decay by a single factor – economy. No matter if all the year round the branch line might carry more milk than passengers from Hemyock to Tiverton Junction, or if the metals from Okehampton to Padstow groaned under the weight of holidaymakers for three months of the year and lay rusting from September to May, only one criterion could be applied when the survival of the West Country railways was at stake – could they pay their way? Thirty years before Dr Beeching came roaring into the West to swing his axe at the branches of the railway tree, the Board of the Southern Railway was shaking its head over the 20 miles of meandering narrow gauge track in the foothills of Exmoor that was known as the Lynton & Barnstaple Railway, and drawing a black ring around Sunday 29 December in its calendar for 1935.

Tourists have been the mainstay of the West Country's economy since the turn of the century. It was the railways that brought in the tourists in such enormous numbers; and the tourists responded by venturing out in their Lanchesters and bullnose Morrises, and turning their backs on the inconvenient timetables and frustrating delays of the local lines, whose stations were often perched several miles from and hundreds of feet above the resorts they were supposed to serve. The railways fought back by laying on bus services between station and town. They built hundreds of ill lit, spartan halts in the countryside. They introduced cheap tickets, and lavatories, meals and drinks on the journey. But the notion of freedom of movement and timing offered by the private car, once tasted, gripped the tourist trade and never let go. The railways gradually fell into decline, appreciated only by local people with no transport of their own and by visiting worshippers at the shrine of steam. One by one the villages, the towns and cities saw the closure notices go up and heard the last train whistling a fading lament. By 1970 only the trunk lines from London and Birmingham that converged on Taunton, the Southern line from London at Exeter and the route onwards south of Dartmoor to Plymouth and Penzance still carried trains, with a few withered arms and fingers poking out here and there to a handful of towns in the rural areas where once the railway was king.

The West Country lines may have gone, but the green paths of their tracks remain. While you can no longer catch the evening train from Halwill Junction to Padstow, you can tramp for three unforgettable days along the track bed that snakes its way south and west behind the cliffs and gorse-strewn hills of the north Cornwall coast. You can wander in autumn among golden oak woods beside the River Teign where iron girder bridges sprouting ferns and moss still carry the single track of the Great Western Railway's Teign Valley Branch across the water. High on the bleak ridge of the Mendips, the ramrods of great mulleins grow in a sheltered cutting of the old Somerset & Dorset Railway. Among the hundreds of miles of disused railways in the south-west are delights for the walker, the naturalist, the railway historian, the holidaymaker – or simply those with a few hours to spare and a love of beautiful and untrodden places.

All you need is a good pair of boots and an Ordnance Survey 1:50,000 map. Every one of the sixteen second series sheets that cover the area carries somewhere among its contours at least one dotted line labelled 'Cse of old rly' that traces the route of a disused railway, showing embankments, cuttings and (usually – but not always accurately) bridges over road and river. Add to these two basic items a set of waterproof over-clothing, a camera, notebook and pencil, and a small haversack, and you are equipped and ready to go.

A little research before the walk will furnish you with details about the history of the particular old railway you have chosen and its place in the local community, the countryside through which it runs and the towns and villages it passes, the men and women who worked in its service and the overall flavour of its birth, life and death. Local libraries in the towns around the old railway may have cuttings sections which chart the intimate details of that line during its life-time and after its closure in a way that neither standard railway histories nor the specialist articles in publications like *The Railway Magazine* can do. A recently formed club, the Railway Ramblers, has undertaken to catalogue and map out the old railways of Britain, to explore them and to record their present state. Its quarterly magazine, *Ramblings*, includes reports on individual lines, advice, news of area meetings and much else. Those who care to contact the club giving news of their explorations or requesting more information can be sure of a warm reception. The address is in Appendix B. A good flower book is an invaluable companion on an old railway walk; nature in all its forms is taking refuge on these peaceful, untouched paths and you are quite likely to see a rare orchid or water plant if you keep a sharp eye open, as well as birds, animals and insects in profusion.

One more piece of research is vital before you start – the times of local buses from the end of your walk back to its starting point! In most rural areas the railways have not been replaced with a comparable bus service. I have usually found it best to park my car at the end of the walk and take the bus to the starting point; this way I avoid a long delay and subsequent bus journey when I am tired and hungry after a long day on the march.

Two notes of caution should be sounded here. The first concerns trespass, a constant thorn in the flesh of old railway walkers. In spite of the assumption by some railway ramblers that 'it all belongs to British Rail and they won't worry about us' the fact is that each old railway line has been chopped up since closure into sections of varying lengths, some owned privately and some still belonging to the British Rail Property Board. The walker is of course expected to gain permission to enter such land. Usually this involves no more than a polite request of the farmer or station owner whose property you want to cross. I have seldom been refused permission to carry on. At most stations the owners are only too pleased to show off their conversions of the buildings and yards into neat houses and gardens with all mod cons, and to expound on the history of their property once they know you are genuinely interested. But as in the case of ordinary hikers and their relationship with landowners, a few thoughtless railway ramblers have made things difficult for everyone else in certain places by their assumption that rights of way exist. On the other side of the coin, bloody-minded farmers and foresters are not unknown! A commonsense approach, asking permission as you go, should ensure a trouble-free ramble.

The other problem springs from the constantly changing nature of the old railway network. One year there may be a derelict station to explore, a bridge spanning the river, a viaduct striding on spindly legs across a valley: the next they may be gone, blown up by gelignite, blown down by a gale, or simply crumbled to dust under the weight of ivy or old age. The unpredictable appearance and disappearance of wildlife adds a welcome touch of mystery to old railway walks; nature generally gives with one hand when it takes with the other. But the slow decay of the peculiarly railway environment has no counter-balancing regenerative process. As the bricks and mortar fall, the cuttings cave in, the cast-iron boundary markers rust away, the railway flavour of the route begins to fade and will not return. The very line of the track itself can be swallowed by a jungle of growth with astonishing rapidity, until only an expert could find the route.

Most of the old railways described in this book have been closed between 15 and 30 years. The atmosphere of the branch line railways is still there for all to see and enjoy, though nowadays they wind unnoticed beside roads, in woods and across remote moorland hills. From Bath to Bournemouth, from Barnstaple to Lynton, from Bovey Tracey to Moretonhampstead, they lie waiting to be explored. As you ramble these old railways of the West Country you will pass through some of Britain's loveliest scenery. You will come across superb examples of the railway architect's art and of the sheer muscle power of the navvies. You may encounter red deer or foxes, buzzards or kingfishers, rosebay willowherb or mugwort. At the very least you will have some fun deciphering your line from the map, and stretch your legs over a few miles of challenging terrain. At best you will enjoy a walk rich in historical associations and absorbing in the variety of its wild life. This book aims to provide a key to the West Country's treasure chest of old railway rambles of every shape and size. Map references for the starting and finishing points of each walk are given in the text.

I have divided the West Country into six areas – the Far West (Cornwall), the Dark Moor (Dartmoor), the Fair Moor (Exmoor), the Mendip Range, the Great Plain (the Somerset Levels and the low lying country to the south) and the Excursion Coast (the branch lines feeding the coastal resorts between Exeter and Bournemouth). Some of the old railways might well have been included in neighbouring areas, as they wind across county boundaries and penetrate different tracts of country. All I can say in defence of my placement of certain borderline cases is that the particular atmosphere of that railway has seemed to me to merit its inclusion in the chosen section. Those who travelled on the line in its working life or who ramble along it nowadays may have other ideas. That is one of the charms of the subject; each individual can make what he will of the abandoned railways and their infinite variety.

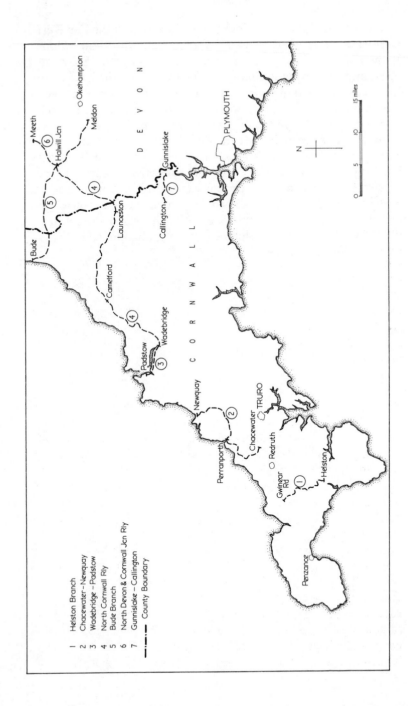

1 Helston Branch
2 Chacewater – Newquay
3 Wadebridge – Padstow
4 North Cornwall Rly
5 Bude Branch
6 North Devon & Cornwall Jcn Rly
7 Gunnislake – Callington
━━ County Boundary

DEVON

CORNWALL

Okehampton
Meeth
Meldon
Halwill Jcn
Bude
Gunnislake
Launceston
Callington
Camelford
PLYMOUTH
Wadebridge
Padstow
Newquay
Chacewater
TRURO
Perranporth
Redruth
Gwinear Rd
Helston
Penzance

N

0 5 10 15 miles

1
THE FAR WEST

The River Tamar rises on the marshy top of Woolley Barrows, a mile below the northernmost border of Cornwall, and for all but a few miles forms the natural and official boundary between Cornwall and Devon. 'Across the Tamar' has signified for Cornishmen down the ages the start of the outside world, whose people may envy but can never measure up to their own strength, industry and fortitude. Based on a shelf of wind-swept granite indented with narrow coves, the rock never far beneath the soil, battered by Atlantic gales, carrying in its heart some of earth's richest deposits of copper and tin, Cornwall has produced a special brand of men: steadfast, insular, hard working and tremendously proud. Nowadays artists and potters, escapers from the big English cities, holidaymakers and restaurateurs have diluted the original moulding. The man who pulls your pint or services your car is likely to greet you in Midland or South London accents; the old dear shuffling down the cobbled street of the fishing village with her basket and shawl has probably just retired from Leeds with her multi-millionaire husband. But the real inhabitants soon make themselves known if the intruder passes a disparaging remark about their county. Centuries of hardship have left the natives of Cornwall with an ever tighter sense of identity, which still binds them together against the outsider in a fashion reminiscent of nationalistic Welsh and Scotsmen.

The most striking symbols of Cornwall's history of desperate poverty and oppression are the ruined engine houses that stand out starkly against the horizon all over the western part of the county. Each gaunt, windowless two or three storey building, with its tall chimney, housed a steam pump that sucked the eternally encroaching water from the bottom of the mines which represented most Cornishmen's only way of earning money. The famous pasties, meat and vegetables in great inch-thick pastry envelopes which are sold in most Cornish pubs and cafés, are a luxurious extension of the scrapings of yesterday's meagre single meal which the wives of the miners baked into a portable pastry case to fortify their men during the long hours spent hacking away naked underground or standing up to the knees in water, squeezing out rags by hand in yet another attempt to keep the working dry. When the miners rebelled against their conditions and marched on the towns, soldiers were used without mercy to beat them back to their place in the underworld. No wonder that families left Cornwall in droves during the eighteenth and nineteenth centuries to seek their fortunes in the new world. 'Cousin Jack' and his few belongings sailed away to fortune or failure, taking with him the narrow, straight and hardy character by which the world knows Cornishmen.

The most famous of Cornish engineers, Richard Trevithick, built steam pumping engines by the score for the mines at the turn of the nineteenth century. He invented fixed engines for extracting the ore from the shafts, and was one of the first to set a steam locomotive running on rails. His steam road carriage scared the daylights out of the denizens of Camborne when it clattered through the streets and overturned spectacularly – though the occupants are reported to have laughed heartily and repaired to a hotel for dinner. His energy and perseverance are the model for Cornishmen everywhere. Yet he, too, was drawn abroad on a wild goose chase after the silver mines of South America, and came home in his declining years to die in poverty and neglect.

The Cornwall that every one of her true sons reckons the pearl of all Britain is a striking county. Not as thickly wooded as Devon, not as lushly grassed as Dorset, not with such variety as Somerset, she possesses in her rocky coves and bays the most impressive coastline in England. Where the inland valleys are sheltered and trees have been able to grow in numbers, as in the Luxulyan valley north-east of St Austell, the walker can find woodland and hill scenery to rival the best of Devon and Somerset. Cornish mining settlements can be grim, but some of the old fishing villages on the southern coast have not yet hidden themselves behind a mask of neon and chips, while such working towns as Redruth, Camborne and St Austell have a flavour unlike any places with similar industries 'across the Tamar'. The Cornish names, too, breathe a kind of cumbersome enchantment to a foreigner's ear – Grumbla, Praze-an-Beeble, Marazanvose and Ventongimps.

The white mountain ranges of quartz slag – the Cornish Alps – and the cratered moonscapes with which the vast china clay works have scarred 25 square miles of countryside near St Austell show clearly the modern Cornishman's attitude to earning his daily bread, as do the all pervading squeak and gibber of electronic games in every bar and café. 3,000 years before the Romans came to Britain, Megalithic barrows and circles were erected all over the moors between Penzance and St Ives. Then as now, Cornishmen knew the chill wind and the hard rock as the basic factors of their lives. In Cornwall they are practical people. The granite is never far beneath the grass.

The Cornwall Railway, built to Isambard Kingdom Brunel's majestic 7ft broad gauge, crossed his tubular masterpiece of a bridge at Saltash in 1859 and ran across his slender timber viaducts to Truro. By 1866 the broad gauge had gained its western outpost, Penzance, and in 1876 was gathered into the all embracing fold of the Great Western Railway. The sick, embittered engineer, worn out by the squabbles which attended the building and launching of his third and greatest steamship, the *Great Eastern*, had died a few months after the opening of the Plymouth to Truro line, but his railway went from strength to strength. The Cornishmen who had been so reluctant to entrust themselves to the Iron Horse became accustomed to steam and speed, and began to come to terms with the foreigners who flocked to their hitherto isolated land. Millions of wagonloads of potatoes and broccoli rattled up the tracks and across the Tamar to the hungry cities of England. For those large, organised fishing fleets who came from strange ports to plunder the Cornish coast, the railway brought prosperity, while the local fishermen lost their trade and their standing in the community. Profound social change has always accompanied the railway, and nowhere with more force than in Cornwall. Yet Cornishmen have used the iron road to transport the precious ores from mine to port since before Waterloo. In 1810 the Poldice tramway carried copper ore from the vast Poldice Mine near St Day along a seven mile route of erratically laid rails to the ships in the harbour at Portreath. Soon other small industrial railways followed – the Redruth & Chasewater (1826), Pentewan (1830) and Bodmin & Wadebridge (1834). Astute railway businessmen began to realise that human freight could be a profitable sideline, and the network of branch lines spread its questing tentacles deeper and deeper into unexplored territory. By 1900 most of the mines were exhausted, and the narrow track beds of their railways already overgrown; but tourism had come bounding in to take the place of industry. The railway managers ran their systems largely for the benefit of through passengers; it was a simple if longwinded journey from Paddington to Penzance, but once the holidaymakers had been decanted with their buckets, spades, and suitcases at Chacewater or Bodmin Road, or Halwill Junction on the London & South Western Railway's route from Exeter, the real delays began. The branch line train for Perranporth, Padstow or Bude might amble in eventually; meanwhile the chugging of the motor car sounded an ever more alluring siren song in the ears of the platform-rooted travellers. Today the main line from Plymouth to Penzance survives, but that early warning to the railway has swelled to an all pervading roar. So congested are the minor roads and lanes that lead to the granite coves and beaches, the fishing villages and market towns, that you can reach these places almost as quickly and a thousand times more pleasantly on foot along the old railways.

1 The Helston Branch

Length: 8¾ miles
Opened: 1887
Closed: Passengers 1962; Goods 1967
OS: 1:50,000 map 203

The most westerly of all walkable disused lines, the Great Western Railway's branch to Helston winds across the West Cornwall plateau from its junction with the main line at Gwinear Road (614384), dodging in and out of the trees, smothered in gorse bushes and brambles, rapidly disappearing back into the landscape. Sustained for a few years after the withdrawal of passenger services by seasonal traffic in broccoli and flowers, it quickly lost the battle with nature once the rails were lifted. Many detours are necessary around the shallow cuttings, where the gorse stabs needles into the thighs and shins of the railway rambler. But it is worth following for the wild beauty of its surroundings.

The old railway can be joined at Carnhell Green as it runs on a ridge among fields of corn and patches of heath, a track surfaced with black granite ballast and bounded by sloe bushes, honeysuckle and foxgloves. At Praze-an-Beeble station site, on the southern edge of the village, one platform remains, and a lamp standard lies across the track. From here to the hamlet of Crowan the old railway has been converted to a tarmac road. Beyond a granite bridge the track becomes extremely jungly and vanishes into the surrounding fields. A $4\frac{1}{2}$ mile post stands out of a hedge. At Skewes Farm, where seagulls cry eternally overhead, the gorse becomes once more impenetrable, and the main road below offers a kinder route into Nancegollan.

Above the station site stands a familiar landmark in this part of Cornwall – a ruined engine house and tall chimney where a pumping engine once drained the mine far below the ground. Nancegollan Station buildings have been razed and the site redeveloped, but the bridge carrying the road over the old railway remains with one stone and one metal span.

Beyond Nancegollan the track passes several farms near Prospidnick; it is hopelessly overgrown but can be followed along the line-side fields and through Trevarno Woods. Truthall Halt, still mentioned on a nearby road signpost, has disappeared in its bushy cutting, but the massive Cober Viaduct spans the valley of the River Cober, a breeze block wall denying access to the walker. Ahead is a good view of Helston on its series of hills.

The line ends above the town at a concrete and earth wall beyond a grey and orange granite engine shed, all that is left of Helston station (662283). Plans to extend the branch south to The Lizard never materialised, but the Great Western Railway began running motor buses from Helston in 1903, and this soon became a thriving business.

Helston is the scene of the famous 'furry dance' each May, when processions of dancers and bands wind in and out of the houses and shops. Sometimes the line is so long that the band at one end is inaudible to the dancers at the other. The town straggles up a hilly main street with tiny alleys leading off each side. Halfway up on the right hand side is the *Blue Anchor* public house, with a little steamy stone brewery in the backyard where strong beer known locally as 'Spingo' is made. It makes a heady end to a hard morning's walk along the gorse-choked branch.

2 Chacewater to Newquay

Length: 18¾ miles
Opened: Chacewater to Perranporth 1903; Perranporth to Newquay
         1905
Closed: 1963
OS: 1:50,000 maps 204 & 200

> 'The Truro & Newquay Railway will, when completed,
> connect, by a fairly direct line, Newquay, the most popular
> summer resort on the north coast of Cornwall, with the
> most popular towns in West Cornwall, and thus facilitate
> traffic that cannot fail to be advantageous to both visitors
> and permanent residents, and will establish a means of free
> intercourse between the different tourist centres, which
> will undoubtedly be greatly appreciated by visitors to
> Cornwall.'
> (*The Railway Magazine* Vol 13, 1903)

The Chacewater to Newquay branch leaves the main Redruth
to Penzance line 1½ miles north west of Chacewater (732455)
and runs due north past Skinner's Bottom and the Wheal Briton
caravan and camping site into Mount Hawke Halt, a good ¾ mile
from the village. The brown brick platform is overgrown with a
fragrant red flowering shrub, sheltering from the Cornish
coastal winds in the gorse-filled cutting – unlike the trees on the
top, which have been blown into tatters.

Beyond Gover's Farm a rough hewn slaty cutting leads past a
brick and granite platelayer's cabin, where the salty wind has
eaten the iron fence posts into weird shapes. The pointed head of
St Agnes Beacon lies ahead and as the line rises there are far
views over to Godrevy Lighthouse and beyond to St Ives. St
Agnes station is a long red-brick building with typical
Edwardian semi-elliptical windows and a rusty canopy. A local
firm of shot-blasters and steelworkers has taken it over. The
town of St Agnes, a mile away, is an old mining centre, and
disused chimneys and workings abound in the region.

From here to Perranporth there is a series of cuttings full of
waist-high gorse and well grown sycamores, interrupted at
Mithian by the impressive Goonbell viaduct with five arches 90ft
high. Perranporth itself thrives on the famous two mile stretch of
Perran beach where the ruins of St Piran's Oratory lie buried in
the sand. Nowadays there are several bustling disco pubs,

thronged streets in the summer, laughter, lights and the smell of well vinegared chips – and over the sands a constant haze from the waves dashing on Ligger Point.

The station is now the premises of a firm of frame housebuilders. The branch follows the valley down to Cocks, where it crosses the river on another viaduct set above woods. Goonhavern station is nothing but a heap of granite lumps and round ended firebricks, with garden-escaped large flowered evening primroses growing amidst the dereliction. Now the gorse clears and the path improves as it curves round to Shepherds, once a busy junction and now a farmyard (where the tiny brick GWR weighbridge hut still stands). Here a mineral line came down from Treamble mines three miles to the north west and ran by East Wheal Rose to Newquay. The portion from Shepherds to Treamble mines, a well made farm road with old 1:40 gradient markers and whistle boards, is easy to follow up to the disused workings. The Newquay branch continues over Penhallow moor on the track of the old mineral mine. Between East Wheal Rose and Benny Halt the track bed again sees trains, and steam trains at that, but they belong to the 15in gauge Lappa Valley Railway which runs as a tourist attraction. Mitchell & Newlyn Halt's concrete strip platform and corrugated iron waiting shed – the

Mitchell & Newlyn Halt (Chacewater–Newquay branch)

bare necessities – stand in the bushes under the scarred face of Newlyn Down. The path undulates past the site of Trewerry & Trerice Halt and curves northwards to join the main Newquay line to Par at a triangular junction, now buried under the new Treloggan industrial estate (824607).

3 Wadebridge to Padstow

Length: 5 miles
Opened: 1899
Closed: 1967
OS: 1:50,000 map 200

The walk begins in Wadebridge a few yards west of the A39 road crossing, at a Cornwall County Council Footpath sign (989725). The old railway runs on the south bank of the Camel estuary, a flat and well gravelled path that hugs the waterside. In places small pockets of Camel water have been trapped by the embankments and separated from the parent river.

There is a constant screaming of seagulls, quacking and calling of water fowl and hum of speed boats. The view is of an ever widening sheet of water that twists and turns among rounded foreshores dotted with trees and white painted houses.

At Penquean the track runs between slate heaps, and the surface becomes rougher as the walk approaches the rusty spider's web of the three span girder bridge over Little Petherick Creek. The wooden decking is rotting away, and there are warning signs which are oddly at variance with the forest of fishing rods that stick out from the piers of the bridge! The detour to the road bridge at Little Petherick and back to the line on the other side of the creek is a good hour's worth of wasted walking. Luckily there are plans to redeck the bridge.

A deep cutting leads into Padstow. The simple, square built station (921751), Waterloo's furthest flung outpost, is now a car park and bus depot with a striking view of the estuary and the sand dunes at Rock across the estuary. The line once extended to the quay, where milepost 259 still stands, a convenient shelf for the glasses of patrons of the pub opposite.

Padstow is celebrated for its May Day Hobby Horse ceremony, its steep and narrow streets and its ban on car parking – a pretty, friendly place full of character. In Edward III's day it sent more ships to the siege of Calais than any other English port except Sandwich, but nowadays only pleasure boats and the famous ferry put out from the harbour. On the branch line's opening day, Padstow let its hair down.

'As the special, with its decorated locomotive, drew into Padstow, the Padstow Artillery and Delabole Brass Bands struck up "See the Conquering Hero Comes", after which Mrs Prideaux Bune, the wife of one of the North Cornwall directors, declared the line open. Even so, Padstow felt that this was not enough, for when, later, the Hon Prideaux Bune was leaving for London, a procession, led by the Artillery Band, marched to the station, where to the sound of exploding detonators, and the tune "A Fine Old English Gentleman", he was presented with a testimonial.' (*The Railway Magazine*, Volume 95, 1949)

4 The North Cornwall Railway (Wadebridge to Meldon Junction)

Length: 54 miles
Opened: Meldon Junction to Halwill 1879; Halwill to Launceston 1886; Launceston to Tresmeer 1892; Tresmeer to Delabole 1893; Delabole to Wadebridge 1895
Closed: 1966
OS: 1:50,000 maps 200, 190, 201 & 191

'The emptying train, wind in the ventilators,
Puffs out of Egloskerry to Tresmeer
Through minty meadows, under bearded trees
And hills upon whose sides the clinging farms
Hold Bible Christians. Can it really be
That this same carriage came from Waterloo?
On Wadebridge Station, what a breath of sea
Scented the Camel valley! Cornish air,
Soft Cornish rains, and silence after steam . . .'
(extract from 'Summoned by Bells' by Sir John Betjeman
– by kind permission of the author)

Wadebridge station (992723), a rotting, crumbling hulk, has come down in the world since a youthful poet waited in the station yard for the brake from Derry's Stable to take him on the last leg of his journey from 31 West Hill, Highgate to Trebetherick on the Camel estuary. From the platform there is a good view of the fifteenth century bridge over the river, before you turn south east to tackle the long and lonely miles of the North Cornwall Railway.

A mile from the station the now disused branch to Bodmin diverges to the right, and the North Cornwall swings left on a girder bridge across the Camel. It forges north east as a well trodden path which traverses a series of deep, shady cuttings, the haunt of several species of butterfly, and runs in fields up to St Kew Highway station, carefully restored and offering bed and breakfast. The North Cornwall Railway's stations are exceptionally sturdy and large, and most are now private houses or business premises.

Rejoining the railway at the bridge in St Kew village, the walker meets the first of a long line of pylons that march in company across the gently undulating countryside. A very damp cutting leads up to the 333yd long Trelill tunnel, the only one on the North Cornwall Railway, that runs right under the village. Local legend says that the tunnel is haunted by the ghost of a man who ended it all with his neck across the rails in the gloomy blackness.

Port Isaac Road station commands a magnificent view of the valley that leads to the tiny resort of Port Isaac, a good 3½ miles away. The track becomes a farm road as it approaches the great cliffs of quarry spoil near Delabole, and runs right beside the lip of the cavernous pit where slate has been quarried and split by hand since Tudor times. Old trackways and a narrow gauge railway line at an angle of 70 degrees plunge down into the depths. The slate company was so keen to be connected to the railway that it gave ¾ mile of its land free to the company. The old station nameboard faces the forlorn blank-eyed building nearby.

Camelford station, two miles further on, is at least neatly maintained as the office of a potato and coal merchant. The town is nearly two miles to the south, while away to the west King Arthur's birthplace, Tintagel Castle, dominates its rocky bay. The North Cornwall line passes Slaughterbridge, where the

Camelford station (North Cornwall Railway)

flower of the Round Table lay heaped in their own blood as Arthur received the fatal blow from his cousin Mordred. Now the railway runs across lonely moorland, the army of pylons forming the only feature in a landscape of sedge and windblown grass; the quartermile posts are in position beside the track, and underline culverts have their own shovel-blade shaped markers.

Otterham station stands on an exposed shoulder of downland, sheltered by a windbreak of tattered trees. Beyond here the line runs in boggy, rough-hewn cuttings where wrens bob around and buzzards wheel overhead. From the completely overgrown cutting at Treskellow the walker must make a road detour by Nether Scarsick and Treglith (a listed house) to Splatt, where Tresmeer station was sited. John Wesley came four times to preach in Tresmeer village.

Tresmeer and Egloskerry stations are in red brick, the latter an immaculate example of sympathetic conversion, with a wonderful garden where the tracks ran, repainted nameboards and barley-sugar lamp-posts.

Unfortunately the line, running in the Kensey valley and close beside the river, is unwalkable from Egloskerry to Launceston because of dense growth of tree saplings, knee deep mud and broken underbridges. Construction of a narrow gauge railway is imminent from Launceston towards Egloskerry. At

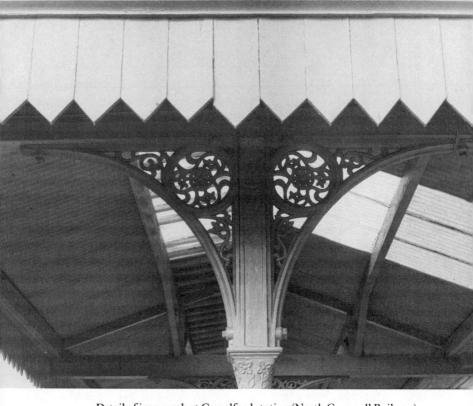

Detail of iron-work at Camelford station (North Cornwall Railway)

New Mills Farm, with its great water wheel ½ mile south of Trewithick Farm, permission can be obtained to walk the last knobbly two miles over thick ballast, if your blisters allow!

The Norman castle and priory ruins at Launceston stick up above the town's steep hill on a green thumb of grassy rock. Launceston was served by two railways; the North Cornwall's station (later London & South Western Railway) has disappeared completely, while the site of the adjacent Great Western Railway establishment is still indicated by a few small ancillary buildings. The day of the opening of the Great Western's branch from Tavistock in 1865 was so rainy that the term 'railway weather' is still used locally to describe dirty weather.

The North Cornwall line crosses over the Great Western's branch on the eastern edge of the town, spans the River Kensey by a three arch stone bridge and curves north for its 14 mile run to Halwill Junction. Most of this section is in the narrow, heavily wooded valley of the River Carey, some of it extremely tough going and in one or two places strictly private; the owner of Tettaridge Barton even sent a squad of toughs in a car to warn me off! The grassy platforms and iron fence entwined with rambling roses at Tower Hill station mark the start of the battle with bracken and broom, gorse and brambles. Milepost 218 stands in the middle of this jungle, bravely maintaining the connection with Waterloo. Dwarf elder scents the cuttings with its strong fragrance.

Beyond Ashwater station, a building of grey stone blocks, the difficult walking conditions gradually ease as the valley opens out, and the track swings round to run into Halwill Junction. This is a desolate spot, high on a windy ridge, where four overgrown track-beds diverge from a central platform on which the low building crumbles quietly. Nearby, clover and birds foot trefoil fill the circle of the station's turntable. Halwill Junction once despatched trains to Torrington, Bude, Okehampton and Padstow, and countless feet have tapped its platform impatiently down the years, waiting for a connection to make its leisurely way out of the dusk. Now the village, still named Halwill Junction, has lost its only garage as well as its railway and wears a silent, deserted air. The Junction Inn, across the road from the station, has a collection of railway photographs and handlamps, and the station's track diagram.

At the opening of the Halwill to Meldon Junction section of the line, the chairman of the North Cornwall Railway said he had never travelled through such a sparsely populated district. Ashbury station, four miles across the moorland plain from Halwill, has been superbly maintained by Mr Smallacombe, the former stationmaster, and his wife, who have lived here for nearly 50 years. Maddaford Moor Halt platform, three miles to the east, stands well down the line from the stationmaster's house, a much extended building where two children of an early incumbent died of pneumonia brought on by the mist-laden air. One end of the house is still clad with the slates that were subsequently hung on the external walls to combat the damp.

The railway threads a plantation of young conifers, with a breathtaking view ahead of the devastation at Meldon Quarry, backed by the hard brown and purple outlines of North Dartmoor. A deep cutting and great embankment on a left-hand curve bring the line round to Meldon Junction (565924), where the North Cornwall Railway meets the disused branch from Okehampton to Lydford and Plymouth. The walk ends at the lofty steel viaduct beside the quarry. From here trains carrying hundreds of tons of stone travel the final $2\frac{1}{2}$ miles into Okehampton.

5 The Bude Branch

Length: $18\frac{1}{2}$ miles
Opened: Halwill to Holsworthy 1879; Holsworthy to Bude 1898
Closed: 1966
OS: 1:50,000 map 190

Bude is unfortunate in the conflict between its aspirations and its geographical position – a well-established resort keen to expand but stuck on a forlorn coast at the end of an interminable road across a fairly featureless plateau. Some fine seaside architecture in its terraces and villas reflects the town's late Victorian blossoming when the railway finally reached it after setting out from Meldon Junction in 1879 and pausing midway for 19 long years at the market town of Holsworthy. That gap in time proved fatal to Bude's hopes for full expansion into a resort to compare with Ilfracombe, and the isolation of this forgotten corner of the West Country has pressed in on the town ever since.

Leaving Halwill Junction (443001) past the abandoned Torrington and Padstow lines, the Bude branch enters three miles of Forestry Commission plantations, running on a series of short embankments and long, deep cuttings, whose floor quickly becomes a peaty swill in wet weather. However, good forest roads offer a handy alternative. Dunsland Cross station, completely isolated, is occupied by several generations of the same family. The branch bends and curves across a heathery moor before a flat stretch beside a tributary of the River Deer leads across the first of Holsworthy's two viaducts into the station. The building is a great gloomy box of a place hung with cold grey slates. Holsworthy is the principal town serving this bleak area, almost all the architecture being heavily Victorian.

Formidable obstacles of barbed wire guard the approaches to the viaduct by which the branch leaves the town, an impressively tall structure over the River Deer with a shovel-blade bridge marker '35' at the eastern end, and glass witness plates over the slowly widening cracks in the concrete walls, marking the inexorable sagging of the viaduct. The track climbs a sharp incline in mossy, damp cuttings where blackberries and hazelnuts tempt the autumnal rambler, and crosses wooded fields into whose steep slopes its formation has been absorbed almost without trace.

At the broken bridge over the Tamar the walker must detour by road to reach Whitstone & Bridgerule station. A brown and cream canopy supported by four ornate pillars stands over a curved platform of sufficient length to accommodate the excursion specials of 10 or more coaches that rumbled towards Bude every summer weekend in railway days.

Now there is an easy walk through open farmland to Helebridge, where the branch has disappeared under the newly widened A39. Beside the track runs the disused Bude canal whose barges were fitted with wheels to enable them to rise up the contours on special inclined planes, a system that did away with the need for conventional locks. Bude Museum has a good display featuring this unique canal, whose reedy course can be followed in an intricate series of wriggling reverse curves from Bude to its terminus at Blagdonmoor Wharf two miles north east of Holsworthy.

The Bude branch accompanies the canal from the A39 for two miles across flat water meadows into the site of Bude Station (211059). Here roses and Michaelmas daisies, from the station garden, compete with sorrel, cow parsley and thistles in the race to smother the platforms. The Bude Development Plan has it marked down as a leisure centre – but the Cornwall Naturalists' Trust is fighting to retain it as a conservation area.

6 The North Devon & Cornwall Junction Light Railway (Halwill Junction to Meeth)

Length: 9 miles
Opened: 1925
Closed: 1965
OS: 1:50,000 maps 190 & 191

Constructed (well after the branch line era) to bridge the gap between Torrington and Halwill Junction, this grandly named line was in fact lightly used by passengers. Its only viable cargo, ball clay, is still shifted northwards to Barnstaple from the quarries at Meeth by rail, long after the intermediate stretch finished its short and undistinguished life.

From Halwill (443001) the walker strikes north, passing the diverging track of the North Cornwall Railway, and then swings east at the bifurcation with the disused line to Bude. The ND & CJLR rambles across Graddon Moor on a falling gradient to the humble stone-built Hole station, a site specially preserved by the Devon Trust for Nature Conservation, and on through attractive farming country to Hatherleigh station, a private house at the far end of an impenetrable cutting where signal masts and lever frame still stand.

A good farm road leads to the girder bridge over the River Torridge and a delightful path in a tunnel of oak trees which emerges from a cutting at Meeth Halt (546079). The tiny three-roomed building, bowed beneath a giant ivy bush, droops on its short platform. The remaining mile up to the railhead is a service road, which runs towards the white hillocks of spoil at Meeth Quarries.

7 The Callington Branch

Length: 4½ miles
Opened: For mineral traffic 1872; Passengers 1908
Closed: 1966
OS: 1:50,000 map 201

Copper, silver, lead, tin, arsenic, granite, bricks, tiles – these and other natural and man-made products poured out of the Tamar Valley mines and works from Saxon times until the early years of this century. Today the district relies on the thousands of little market gardens that form a patchwork on the river valley slopes, a traditional industry since the days when Nelson's navy gobbled up all the fresh produce the area could supply.

In 1872 the East Cornwall Mineral Railway opened up its seven mile line from Calstock Quay, a few miles up-river from Plymouth, to the mining settlement of Kelly Bray, a mile north of Callington; 36 years later, the local people took their first legal trip along the branch. By then the mines had closed and the railway was already dying on its feet.

A marvellous introduction to the walk is a ride by train from Plymouth up the contorted single line branch to Gunnislake, looping round over the rivers on immense viaducts before disembarking at the dilapidated station (427711). Once through the first gorse-strewn section, there is pleasant walking amid bracken and heather past ruined engine houses to the platform of Chilsworthy station, a peaceful spot if one can ignore the monstrous quarry clattering away on the left. Stepping stones across a wet patch of track lead on to Latchley station, an attractive building now privately occupied, with a 6½ milepost on one platform and a pillar box marked 'Latchley Station'.

Seven Stones Halt, two miles further on, was built in 1910 to cater for trippers who brought their picnics up to the swingboats on Hingston Down. Now a cab roof marked 'Refreshments' on the rubbish dump near the deserted platform provides the railway rambler's only solace on a hot day.

The Callington branch snakes along the northern flank of Hingston Down, past Luckett station (an identical building to Latchley, and also a private house) and terminates 640ft above sea level. The site of Callington station, actually situated at Kelly Bray (362715), has been flattened and is a wide open space.

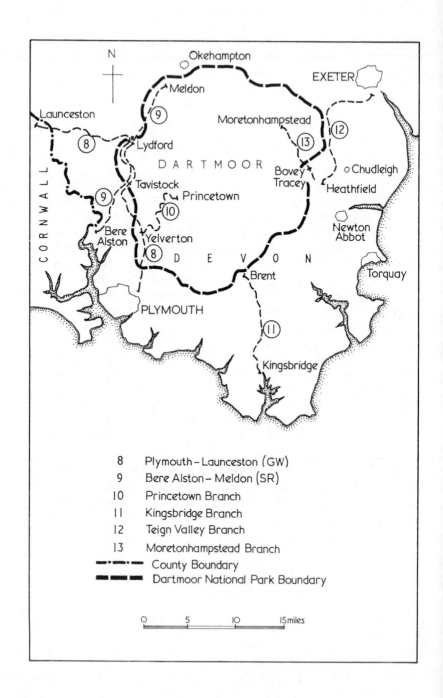

8	Plymouth – Launceston (GW)
9	Bere Alston – Meldon (SR)
10	Princetown Branch
11	Kingsbridge Branch
12	Teign Valley Branch
13	Moretonhampstead Branch
▬·▬·▬·	County Boundary
▬ ▬ ▬	Dartmoor National Park Boundary

2

THE DARK MOOR

A line drawn north-westward from Exeter to the market town of Okehampton, and from there running south-west through Tavistock and south to Plymouth, hems in a rough square of South Devon characterised by steep valleys with villages clinging to the river banks and thousands of acres of ancient woodland. On the strip of coastline that faces south and east to Torbay and Start Bay are some of the busiest West Country seaside resorts – Torquay, Paignton and Brixham. The channel coast shelters scores of smaller towns and villages, backed by gently swelling hills threaded with narrow lanes, whose hedges bend inland before the eternal sea wind.

Rising from the heart of this corner of Devon are the granite and peat wastes of a great hump of land which throughout history has attracted, ground down and finally repelled the farmers and miners who tried to exploit it. Dartmoor is one of Britain's oldest and wildest tracts of country, a sopping sponge of moss, peat and water across which sudden mists descend to blot out all landmarks and leave the benighted traveller more lost and alone than in any other part of the West. Nowadays the desolate stretches of the moor are barren ground, riddled with the cartridge cases and shell craters of the army, nibbled at by sheep and lamented in the mournful bubbling call of curlews and mewing of buzzards. There are few tracks across Dartmoor which an inexperienced walker would care to follow in bad weather, and even on the sunniest day the moor holds an atmosphere of menace. In his account of his walk from Land's End to John O'Groats, *Journey Through Britain*, John Hillaby calls it 'the Dire Moor'. As he got lost in a Dartmoor mist and was nearly swallowed by the quivering mud of Cranmere Pool he has some justification for that grim title. Compared with the springy turf, many trees and rolling hummocks of Exmoor, the bare rocks and hard purple outlines of Dartmoor seem to warn rather than entice the outsider.

Perhaps because of this isolation and the forbidding expanses of wet heather and peat, parts of the moor can be stunningly beautiful. The walker is unlikely to meet many other explorers, once away from the two main roads (B3357 and B3212) that intersect the moor, meeting at Two Bridges in the centre. Under a blue sky, with cloud shadows chasing each other across the granite outcrops, Dartmoor certainly has grandeur. For a solitary ramble hard in the face of the natural elements there is nothing to touch it in this corner of the West Country – until the mist closes in!

The remnants of iron age settlements, scattered all over the slopes, bear eloquent witness to the conditions on Dartmoor. The circular foundations of these huts, a few feet across, each have a right-angled entrance tunnel facing the south and west, away from the icy winds and rain. When the harsh climate drove these early subsistence farmers down into the valleys, no one was hardy enough to take their place. Tin miners set up small habitations from which they worked in excruciating discomfort, and the towns and villages below the moor grew fat on the sweat of their brows. At one time the tin communities virtually ruled themselves, their Stannary Courts dealing out rough justice to offenders against their laws. But the Dartmoor weather and the unyielding terrain have combined to keep men off the moor to the present day.

Round the edges of the moor, and in the country to the south and east, things are very different. The valleys of the Teign and the Bovey, the Dart and the Avon are well forested, snug and lovely. There are old market towns which absorb the summer influx of tourists without losing their own individuality – Totnes and Kingsbridge are good examples. Visited at Easter or in the autumn, the coastal villages are uncrowded. At Hope Cove or Slapton you can catch the flavour of small communities that have their own life and work, independent of the outside world. Plymouth is a great city, the bustling capital of South Devon where people still pass the time of day with strangers. The rivers Lynher, Tamar, Tavy, Plym and Yealm meet the sea in or around Plymouth, and it is a city of many waterfronts. Tudor pubs, ships' chandlers, maritime warehouses and the square, plain magnificence of the buildings of the Royal William Victualling Yard rub shoulders with modern developments planned after the heart of the city was torn out in wartime bombing raids.

South Devon was the scene of the ignominious failure of one of the most imaginative innovations of the great Isambard Kingdom Brunel, whose ideas and engineering genius opened up so many new possibilities for the Victorians. In 1847 the inhabitants of the coastline between Exeter and Newton Abbot marvelled over long miles of pipeline that had been laid by the navvies along the mainline railway. Soon they were to marvel even more – for curious trains began to shuttle between the two towns, trains with no engines! Brunel's active brain had conceived the atmospheric system, whereby a piston fixed to the driving carriage and running in the pipeline propelled the train along the tracks, sucked by the vacuum created by pumping stations along the line. But alas! Technology had not advanced far enough to keep pace with invention. The continuous leather flap over the slit in the pipe where the piston arm emerged, necessary to maintain the vacuum, perished and rotted – and by 1848 the idea was dead. The railways, however, steamed on. The main line reached Plymouth the same year, and branches began to proliferate in the valleys.

Granite, slate and china clay had been carried from their workings on Dartmoor to lower ground by tramways since 1820, when the Haytor Tramway opened near Bovey Tracey. The granite sleepers marking its course can still be traced on foot. Three years later the Plymouth & Dartmoor Railway carted granite, goods and passengers to and from Princetown. Cann Quarry in the woods above Plymouth had its own line by 1829, parts of which can also be walked between the trees as far as Plym Bridge. Two tramways in particular make excellent railway rambles, being still clearly marked out on the ground. One of these is the Redlake Tramway, opened in 1911 and closed when the clay company went broke in 1932, which runs from Bittaford near Ivybridge north for seven and a half miles to the abandoned workings at Redlake. The line is flat and easy underfoot, with fine views of the moor all round. A few miles to the west is the Lee Moor Tramway, which was opened in 1858, 53 years before the Redlake Tramway, and outlasted it by 15 years. This four mile line runs from its junction at Plym Bridge with the Cann Quarry Tramway up to the extensive china clay works on Lee Moor, and includes two steep inclines which were worked by cables.

The passenger railway lines, meanwhile, were slowly and

steadily opening up the moor and its surrounding countryside. A few of them have not found their way into this chapter: the six mile branch from Plymouth to Yealmpton (opened in 1898 and closed to passengers in 1947 – Yealmpton's claim to fame is that 'Old Mother Hubbard' was written here by the sister-in-law of local worthy Squire Bastard): the two mile Brixham line which from 1860 to 1963 stood as a living monument to the perseverance of one Brixham man, R. W. Wolston, and his determination to have his native town connected to the main line: the Ashburton branch, whose track from Totnes now carries the Dart Valley steam trains. Of these, the Yealmpton and Brixham branches can be followed most of the way on foot. Rambles along the other abandoned railways on the Dark Moor and in its shadow will lead you through some of the loneliest and loveliest country in this part of England.

8 From Plymouth to Launceston by Great Western Railway

Length: 31¾ miles
Opened: Plymouth to Tavistock 1859; Tavistock to Launceston 1865
Closed: Passengers 1962
OS: 1:50,000 map 201

> 'Down along the valley the smoke is rising,
> There where the green fields meet the woods,
> Chugging up to Coryton, struggling up to Liddaton,
> Working like a Trojan comes the Lan'son goods.'

Straggling up the river valleys, skirting the western flank of Dartmoor and suddenly veering off into the back of beyond, the Great Western Railway's branch line from Plymouth to Launceston makes a wonderful two day ramble with a variety of splendid views of woodland, moor and farmland. It represented a notable victory for the South Devon Railway, which got its broad gauge metals to Tavistock a good 30 years before the London & South Western Railway finally arrived to compete for the Plymouth traffic with the standard gauge.

The walk is best started at Plym Bridge (524587), a noted beauty spot 1½ miles upstream from Tavistock Junction where the branch leaves the main Great Western line to Plymouth. A clear track meanders up Bickleigh Vale through the oak and birch woods, superb in autumn in their coats of many colours.

The railway crosses deep, rocky ravines on tall viaducts, and as the valley goes northwards there are glimpses of rolling farmland and the humpy wastes of Dartmoor to the east.

To the right of the first of these viaducts is Cann Quarry. Its enormous height and ruggedness can best be appreciated from below. It was served by its own tramway whose course can be followed through the woods from Marsh Mills. Two more viaducts lead to Bickleigh station, a flat expanse of grass, near which you may notice a hammering noise among the trees – not a mad blacksmith, but the commandos of nearby Bickleigh Barracks at play.

Shaugh Bridge Platform, sited directly below a road bridge, was provided for picnickers from Plymouth bound for Shaugh Bridge, where the waters of the rivers Cad and Meavy meet to form the River Plym. Twenty thousand day trippers took the little branch train every Bank Holiday in the railway's heyday. Beyond the halt, an iron aqueduct conducts the Devonport Leat over the line at the dark entrance to Shaugh Tunnel. Tunnelophobes can take a convenient detour to the right which leads to Clearbrook Halt. From here on the track is emphatically private property, but from the road bridge over the Meavy a footpath takes the walker through the woods to Yelverton station, where the stationmaster's house is occupied and restored. A few hundred yards up the road into Yelverton is the Rock Hotel, an unspoilt example of a Dartmoor pub – friendly, rambling and stained by centuries of tobacco smoke. Here I heard an elderly local character holding forth about his life: 'I used to sleep with a girl at Torquay – but she ran off with a rotter!'.

The track of the branch to Princetown (page 41) runs off to the right on its misty moorland meanderings. Yelverton tunnel on the Launceston branch dives under the road, but the track can be picked up again at Horrabridge station by crossing the common on Roborough Down on a well marked path. The station layout contains platforms, sidings and two strongly built stone sheds.

A grassy track crosses Magpie viaduct, with wider views of the valleys running up rowards Tavistock, and suddenly dips downhill on a huge 45 degree slope at the site of Walkham viaduct – 376yd long and 132ft high. It was one of the last of Brunel's timber viaducts, standing until well into this century before being replaced by an iron girder structure. After sweating up the embankment on the other side of the River Walkham, you can walk through the tunnel under Grenofen village; a pleasant alternative is a path on the left bank of the wide, shallow river which leads to a bridge and a very steep minor road into Grenofen.

The branch runs on embankments up to Tavistock, whose houses cluster on the hills ahead. The long platform at Whitchurch Halt is covered in sweet peas, escaped from gardens which block the path on the outskirts of the town.

Tavistock South is partly a factory site with the remainder obliterated by road works; the Great Western Railway station with its overall roof and ancillary buildings have disappeared. But on opening day, 21 June 1859, the *Tavistock Gazette* gave the railway due honour. It reported that the town's welcoming procession included John Eddy, aged 98, and Maud Doidge, 97, in the Portreeve's carriage, Bakers in a Waggon, working at an Oven, exhibiting a large loaf as an Emblem of the Staff of Life, Woolcombers on a Waggon, with Combe Pot, all in full work, and Tavistock Fife and Drum Band.

'The rear was brought up by a group of people of all sorts, sizes and conditions . . . it is needless to say that the procession hardly took the form allotted in the programme . . . there was scarcely a window or a roof ledge through the various streets but which had its occupants, and altogether the scene appeared one of unalloyed enjoyment . . . the day's festivities included a public luncheon, sports, a public tea, and a grand display of fireworks by the late Mr. Monk.'

On closing day (Saturday 29 December 1962) the last train to Launceston was attended by rather less pomp and circumstance. A full blizzard was blowing, and the train arrived in Tavistock, $15\frac{3}{4}$ miles from Plymouth, 5 hours and 20 minutes late, unable to turn another wheel. The stranded passengers completed their journeys during the following day as best they could. *The Railway Magazine*, with masterly understatement, reported this heroic anti-climax under the heading 'Inclement End to West Country Branch'.

The LSWR's Bere Alston to Okehampton branch straddles the valley on a viaduct which dominates the town, and soon the Great Western Railway meets it and runs in tandem for the next seven miles to Lydford. Great rivalry existed between the

On the left, the Great Western – on the right, the London & South Western (between Tavistock and Lydford, West Dartmoor)

companies, and continued among staff of British Railways Southern and Western Regions. Many are the hair-raising tales of races between engine drivers along this section, where the tracks run only a few feet apart. Separate bridges were built for the two lines, and four miles north of Tavistock two stations stand within a mile or so of each other – the imposing Brentor station of the LSWR and the tiny Mary Tavy & Blackdown Halt of the GWR – both serving an almost deserted region. Back to back march the boundary markers of the rival companies in the no-man's-land between the two track beds, relics of a battle that history has declared an honourable draw. Whichever path you choose – the Great Western is well grassed but boggy, the London & South Western wide but thickly ballasted – the volcanic upthrust of Brentor, topped by the church of St Michael de Rupe, calls you on towards Lydford, where the once busy station platforms are doing their best to fade away under weeds.

The LSWR forges ahead towards Okehampton, while the Great Western track swings away to the left and runs for nearly three miles on the outskirts of some of the loveliest woodland in the West Country, the Lydford Forest. The River Lyd courses through the woods, its gurgling compensating for the sudden disappearance of the dramatic outline of Dartmoor, now at the walker's back. Seven river crossings have to be made between Lydford and Launceston, and most of the bridges are gone. The first is between Liddaton Halt and Coryton station, where an

Lifton church, framed in the arch of a mineral line that crossed the GWR Launceston branch

upper storey has been cleverly added to the original building. In 1972 the whole site was put on the market by BR at just £2,500!

The Launceston branch runs on across the River Lew by an intact footbridge, and threads the grounds of Sydenham House which can be seen between the trees on the left. A graceful iron bridge spans the track, and just up the bank is a Great Western Railway boundary marker of 1895. There are two more river crossings before Lifton station, now occupied by the vast complex of the Ambrosia Creamery. A level crossing gate stands near the brick arch which took a tramway over the line, and through which Lifton church is neatly framed on its hill. Seeds of ragwort and rosebay willowherb have blown up into cracks in the brickwork and sprouted into plants 15ft from the ground.

The old railway runs on across flat fields on the edge of Lifton Park with a view ahead of Launceston on its great hill. It crosses the Lyd twice and the Tamar once (detours are necessary) and passes under the North Cornwall line before entering a narrow, overgrown cutting which leads into the site of Launceston's GWR station (331851). Passenger services were diverted to the SR station in 1952, and the GWR station eked out its last few years as a goods depot – now only a couple of red brick huts tell the tale.

9 From Plymouth to Meldon Viaduct through the Tamar Valley

Length: 16 miles
Opened: 1890
Closed: 1968
OS: 1:50,000 map 201 & 191

Bere Alston, the starting point of this walk, can be reached by train along the charming Gunnislake branch — how long before it, too, falls to the axe? From the station (442674) the London & South Western Railway's line strikes out north east through a series of overgrown cuttings to reach the Tamar on the edge of the river valley above Double Waters, where the River Walkham flows down from Horrabridge to join the Tavy. The old railway snakes along at the top of the valley in lovely wooded scenery, passing through Shilla Mill tunnel before crossing a tall viaduct over the River Lumburn and another over the town before reaching the site of Tavistock North station. Narrow streets huddle close beneath the LSWR viaduct, one of the most impressive features of the town.

The track runs on a narrow path with a steep drop on the right down to the main A386 Okehampton Road. Soon it meets the Great Western branch to Launceston, and the rival companies forge north in close attendance for the next seven miles to Lydford, as described on pages 36 to 37.

At Lydford station's bushy platforms they part company. The Okehampton line can be followed along the eastern edge of the town, but few walkers would want to miss the nearby trail through the Lydford Gorge. Whitelady Falls plummets down a shining rock funnel in a 100ft sheer column at the bottom of this tree-lined cleft which the Lyd has carved out over the centuries, and there are low and high level paths through the gorge which emerge by Lydford Castle. The castle was built in 1195 to house offenders against the savage Stannary (tin mining) laws.

'Oft have I heard of Lydford law —
How in the morn they hang and draw
And sit in judgement after . . .'

In St Petrock's churchyard a monument to a local watchmaker, George Routleigh, carries this apt inscription –

> '. . . wound up
> In hopes of being taken in hand by his Master
> And of being thoroughly cleaned and repaired
> And set a-going
> In the world to come.'

Beyond Lydford the track runs in a long right-hand cutting, containing a rusty tin 'Catch Points' notice, up to Bridestowe station, now being restored. The Edwardian stationmaster here took great pride in the topiary he practised on his display of shrubs. From the station there are wide views – two great tors ahead and rolling farmland all round.

Soon the track of a $4\frac{1}{2}$ mile mineral line to Kitty Tor leaves the branch on the right. The LSWR, supporting a fine colony of broom bushes, passes wind-scoured Sourton church (the Devil is supposed to have died of cold on Sourton Moor) and becomes a dilapidated tarmac road before its junction with the North Cornwall Railway's line to Halwill Junction and points west, a few hundred yards short of the great steel Meldon Viaduct (565924).

10 The Princetown Branch

Length: $10\frac{1}{2}$ miles
Opened: 1883
Closed: 1956
OS: 1:50,000 maps 201, 202 & 191

> '. . . Through the rock
> Of aged hills abrupt, and caverns deep
> The Railway leads its mazy track. The will
> Of Science guides its vast meanders on
> From Plym's broad union with the ocean wave
> To Dartmoor's silent desert; and the depths
> Of solitudes primeval now resound
> With the glad voice of man. The dauntless grasp
> Of industry assails yon mighty Tors
> Of the dread wilderness, and soon they lift
> Their awful heads no more.'

This moorland railway was built in high hopes of opening up the Dark Moor. In fact its main traffic was prisoners, prison warders and prison goods bound to and from the grim jail at Princetown, together with a little granite from the Dartmoor quarries. It closed in the same manner in which it lived much of its life – in a thick mist, hardly noticed by the outside world.

The line should be joined at the south eastern corner of Dousland (543678), whose stationmaster's house is now the Post Office. The track is perfectly clear underfoot all the way to Princetown; only lichen and fungi can find a hold here on the bare moor. Burrator Halt, opened in 1924 to cater for the tourists, still has its two sets of steps and a platform base hidden in the bracken. The line twists and turns, strewn with iridescent flakes of granite, gaining height through the Forestry Commission plantation above Burrator Reservoir. Apart from the bleating of sheep, hardly a sound can be heard.

Above Horseyeatt Farm the railway enters the open moor – beware of the bulls! The branch was built largely over the track of a much earlier line – the Plymouth & Dartmoor Railway of 1823 – and the original granite sleepers pierced by bolt holes can be seen beside the track. Soon you pass the site of Ingra Tor Halt, go under the massy granite arch of the only overbridge on the line, and make a two mile horseshoe sweep round the quarries and sidings at King's Tor before returning to a point a couple of hundred yards from where the horseshoe began but at a higher elevation! King Tor Halt must have been one of the loneliest places on any railway in England. Heather, peat hags, granite outcrops and the mounds of pre-historic habitations are all around; and a profound silence reigns. One solitary farm clings to the hillside among its few shelter trees. From here the course of the line can be seen as far back as the granite bridge.

Winding on beneath the slim pencil of a TV mast, the path approaches Princetown with a view ahead of the tall chimneys of the jail. Dartmoor Prison was built in 1806 on a site donated by the Prince of Wales (hence the name Princetown) at the suggestion of Sir Thomas Tyrwhitt, the instigator of the old Plymouth & Dartmoor Railway, to house the prisoners taken in the Napoleonic wars. The sole remains of Princetown station (588735), 1,400ft above sea level, are a derelict slate-hung shed and an old Great Western Railway 'Private Road' sign, snapped in half.

11 The Kingsbridge Branch

Length: 12½ miles
Opened: 1893
Closed: 1963
OS: 1:50,000 map 202

The Great Western Railway Kingsbridge branch hugs the banks of the River Avon for eight of its 12½ miles, and crosses the river 10 times. As half the bridges are gone, there are some detours to be made through the woods, but the beauty of the tree-lined valley makes up for the inconvenience.

The track is best joined at Avonwick (716583), a mile south of the junction with the main Newton Abbot to Plymouth line. Avonwick station, a solid grey stone house with rectangular granite framed windows and square topped chimneys like the others on the branch, is owned by Bob Gale; he suffers from inconsiderate trespassers in the holiday season, but will gladly show courteous ramblers the excellent conversion he has carried out – and sell them a book about the railway when they leave. Moreover he is in the bed and breakfast business so you can stay at a real GWR station!

You should cross to the right-hand bank of the river before the broken bridge, and follow the track through the woods on an overgrown but negotiable path. Wrens and woodpeckers abound, and the river gurgles below the line in its tunnel of trees.

Two more broken bridges lead to Gara Bridge station, just by the narrow medieval packhorse bridge. The owner has been waiting for years for planning permission to extend the station building across the track bed; meanwhile he has made a snug camp in the storeshed. If you stick to the left-hand bank of the river you can pick up the track again in Storridge Wood, whence it can be walked between high hillsides, gorgeous in autumn, to Topsham Bridge, then abandoned for a riverside path on the left of the river, resumed below the ancient farmstead of Wood Barton, and pursued onwards to Loddiswell station, another private house perched above the road.

One and a half miles of climbing to the south is Sorley tunnel (638 yards), a straight bore beneath the hamlet of Sorley. Part of the formation on embankments has been bulldozed away. The old railway curves south and crosses the A379 on the outskirts of Kingsbridge, although housing estates occupy the line both sides of the A379 bridge. The terminus (731442) is an industrial estate of corrugated asbestos barns, each housing a separate concern. The long stone station building stands at the south end, facing out towards the Kingsbridge estuary over the slate-hung houses of the town.

12 The Teign Valley Railway

Length: 16½ miles
Opened: Heathfield to Ashton 1882; Ashton to Exeter 1903
Closed: Passengers 1958
OS: 1:50,000 maps 192 & 191

This is a breathtaking woodland walk in an unfrequented valley, its pleasures enhanced by the continued existence of three of the four bridges over the River Teign.

Half a mile south of Exeter St Thomas station the branch curves south west off the main Plymouth line and runs as sidings and then beside a new road development (914905), cut in two by the A30 dual carriageway before reaching the unspoilt little village of Ide. The line crosses a heron-haunted valley on a bushy embankment and plunges into the oak woods. The next five miles are a succession of embankments and cuttings with about 25 bridges and 30 culverts – not to mention two tunnels. The purple earth of the fertile Devon fields is interspersed with thickly wooded hillsides and the roofs of farmsteads far below the line.

The 829yd Perridge tunnel was built to hide the offensive sight of the trains from the owner of Perridge House, which stands in parkland above the railway looking east over a magnificent panorama of woodland. Deadly red and white spotted fly agaric mushrooms grow in the cutting, and fungi of a more edible sort are cultivated in the darkness of the tunnel.

On the far side the railway runs through the Culver estate, home of the Eden family. Longdown station was carefully restored by an enthusiast who repainted the signs and put up railway posters. Then he left the district, and his handiwork is slowly being eroded by nature and vandals. The lady who lives at the stationmaster's house remembers the beautiful rose beds on the platform with 'G.W.R.' picked out in white-washed stones. The train crews usually delivered the morning papers at isolated farms along the line in exchange for a rabbit or two. The guard operated a rigid class system – grammar school children were allotted their own carriage, while 'layabouts' from the state secondary schools were put in another, away from the swots!

The Teign Valley branch runs through the 251yd Culver Tunnel, excavated to placate the Edens, swings from west to south and drops down a steep gradient to river level at Leigh Cross. Here it becomes impassable, but can be rejoined at Christow station, a neat bungalow with gas lamps marking out the platforms. The station bridge has a 4ft gangway added at the side for pedestrians.

The track runs on the left bank of the Teign, curves below a huge razor-back slope and crosses the river on an intact girder bridge before halting at the line's only broken bridge. A road detour brings the walker to Ashton station, a small single-storey building in candy coloured brick with a rusty water pumping wheel in the garden. Buzzards mew above the woods, and a long patch of Himalayan balsam grows beside the river – purple flowers with an upper hood-like petal turned back to expose a green tongue and spotted throat. The bristling chimneys and windows of Canonteign House are framed by trees high up on the right. Sir Edward Pellew, in fiction the steadfast friend and patron of Captain Horatio Hornblower, in fact built the house in 1820 and left an enormous Elizabethan mansion to crumble away. Whitcombe sidings, running from two flooded quarry pits on the left, lead to a road crossing where a damp, ivy-smothered engine shed is now a garage.

Beyond Trusham station, another candy coloured bungalow, the line crosses the river and enters a desolation of crackling pylons, corrugated iron sheds and stacks of concrete pipes among which scurry forklift trucks. The clatter of quarry machinery drowns the sound of Teign water and chirruping birds. The old railway crosses the river on a bridge whose piers have arrow-shaped feet, pointing into the flow of water to lessen its erosive effect. With ballast underfoot, the walker passes railway wagon bodies in the fields before meeting the A38 motorway embankment. On the far side, Chudleigh station and Chudleigh Knighton Halt lie under the new road formation, but from Knighton Heath the track can be followed over the Teign to its junction with the Moretonhampstead branch (833762) at Heathfield station.

13 The Moretonhampstead Branch

Length: 7 miles
Opened: 1886
Closed: Passengers 1959
OS: 1:50,000 map 191

From Heathfield trainloads of clay still go away south to Newton Abbot, but just north of the station the rails peter out (823769) and the track runs north westwards to Bovey Tracey. It passes the old Bovey Pottery with its three bottle-kilns, and a forgotten halt, before reaching Bovey station.

The branch becomes a public footpath through the oak woods of the Bovey valley, rising steeply to an abrupt full stop at a broken road bridge. Spring clips and fishplates, scattered by the demolition gang that dismantled the railway, dot the ballast. The River Bovey swings away, but a tributary takes over and accompanies the line all the way to Moretonhampstead.

The branch skirts the lovely village of Lustleigh which clings to the 'cleave' cut in the hills by the river. In a 1934 film version of the *Hound of the Baskervilles*, the pocket-size London detective Lestrade alighted at Lustleigh station to join Holmes and Watson in their showdown with the Hound. Evocative descriptions of the railway in Victorian days can be found in *Small Talk at Wrayland* by Cecil Torr, who lived a mile away. Nowadays the once beautiful station garden is a mass of weeds.

From this point the walk becomes a struggle through dense woodland undergrowth, rewarding for its quietness, the seldom seen aspects of the river, the profusion of fungi and the sheer pleasure of breaking new ground – but watch out for some broken bridges over forest tracks!

Below Wray Barton the branch emerges from the trees for a clear run up to two broken bridges over the A382. Beyond the second of these, Moretonhampstead station (758857) is the headquarters of a road transport firm. Here lorries are repaired in the handsome stone engine shed and the big goods shed is their storage depot – a neat example of old usage into new. The market town of Moretonhampstead is the social centre for this part of Dartmoor. Another Conan Doyle hero, Brigadier Gerard, would approve of the preservation in the church porch of the tombstones of some of his gallant compatriots who died here while on parole from Dartmoor Prison.

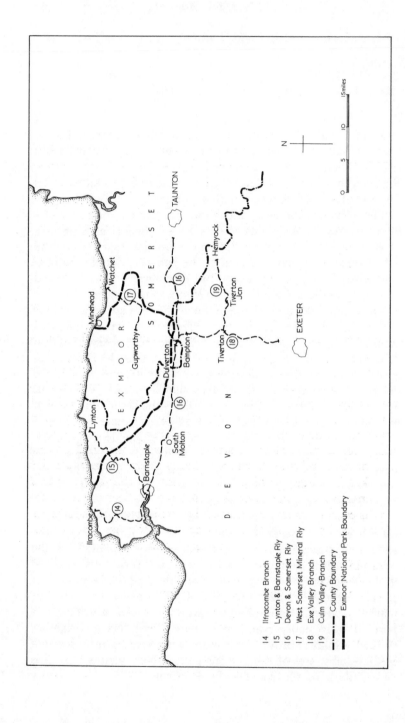

N

0 5 10 15 miles

TAUNTON

Hemyock

⑲

Tiverton
Jcn

EXETER

⑯

Tiverton

⑱

Bampton

Dulverton

⑯

South
Molton

Barnstaple

⑮

Ilfracombe

⑭

Lynton

E X M O O R

Gupworthy

⑰

Watchet

Minehead

S O M E R S E T

D E V O N

14 Ilfracombe Branch
15 Lynton & Barnstaple Rly
16 Devon & Somerset Rly
17 West Somerset Mineral Rly
18 Exe Valley Branch
19 Culm Valley Branch
— · — · County Boundary
━ ━ ━ Exmoor National Park Boundary

3

THE FAIR MOOR

Perhaps it is the sandstone, warm and soft, which underlies Exmoor that makes its overall flavour so different from the forbidding desolation of grey granite Dartmoor. Where the underlying rocks outcrop they are red and brown, cheerful colours of earth that make an exhilarating contrast to the heather and dun grass of the upland moors or the green expanses of grazing land that form a protective belt around Exmoor's bare crown. Exhilaration is the word that best describes the walker's reaction to the Fair Moor – where Dartmoor speaks of lashing rain and creeping mist, of echoes and emptiness, Exmoor brings hopes of blue skies, of larks singing and tractors grunting in the red ploughed fields far below, of immense views over the green shoulders of the hills into wooded combes that lead off the moor's top to the sea.

Trees are a feature of this great National Park, 'Exmoor Forest' by title and in some places almost a forest in fact. Any place where the King's special hunting laws applied in medieval times was designated 'forest', but there were very few trees here until the nineteenth century. Now every combe (the local name for a cleft where a stream escapes from underground confinement and runs down the flanks of the hills) boasts a collar of oak, ash or beech, which helps to maintain the variety of bird and animal life on the moor. Stag hunting has been practised for centuries, and hereabouts the red deer still clings precariously to his last toe-hold in England. Opponents of the chase argue for his retention in peace, while supporters claim that his race would long ago have been wiped out by the farmers whose crops he despoils if the hunt did not exercise control over his numbers.

Exmoor extends for some 200 square miles on a long line running south east from Combe Martin on the north coast to Dulverton on the River Exe, and thence roughly north to Minehead. This tract of open land, slashed by deep valleys and threaded by innumerable streams, was inhabited long before the Romans, as witness a wealth of barrows, stone circles and hill forts. Ancient British tribes mined iron and copper on the moor, and seem to have survived in more comfort and prosperity than the miserable huddlers upon the Dark Moor. Yet Exmoor was a lawless and wild place until recent times – R. D. Blackmore's gang of blood-thirsty Doones is an accurate portrayal of many of the sheep rustlers and robbers who concealed themselves in the fastnesses of hidden valleys and lived as they liked, independent of national law and order. Few roads crossed the moor, though a multitude of tracks and drove roads led in and out of the stone walled sheep runs. Barnstaple to the west had been a prosperous wool centre for centuries, South Molton a small market town; but no other settlement in or near the moor amounted to more than a handful of houses and a few hundred inhabitants.

Then came the railways. Barnstaple was linked to the outside world in 1854 by the North Devon Railway line from Exeter, though the town still remained curiously isolated from the rest of the county. In 1855 it pushed out another branch south west towards Bideford. The Devon & Somerset limped across the southern foothills of Exmoor to Barnstaple in 1873. The following year Ilfracombe welcomed the railway and began to put on a late spurt of development as a seaside resort; and in 1898 the tiny coastal village of Lynton followed suit. In 1908 the Bideford, Westward Ho! & Appledore Railway reached Appledore. This individualistic light railway, with its American style coaches and engines fitted with cowcatchers is not described here, though its course can be followed for most of the way. Barnstaple now had no fewer than five separate lines of railway radiating from its hub in all directions, and seemed set for expansion and prosperity in line with the other regional railway centres of Britain. But somehow it never happened. The tourists came in the summer in their hundreds of thousands, but they could not make up for the hungry out-of-season months when farmers, school children and women with their marketing baskets made up the passenger list. Slowly the system began to die. Today the first railway to reach Barnstaple is the only one still open – the others are left to the undergrowth, the red deer and the railway rambler.

This chapter spreads its net far and wide to draw the disused railways under the umbrella of the Fair Moor. The Brendon Hills, on the eastern flank of Exmoor, are admitted for their geographical position; though the bleak isolation of their wild spaces, riddled with mines and almost uninhabited, has little in common with Exmoor's great uplift. Up the sheer face of the Brendons struggles the track of the West Somerset Mineral Railway, that attracted a nucleus of civilisation around its stations until the iron ore ran out. The Exe Valley line, starting just north of Exeter and winding its way beside the River Exe, penetrates the moor near Dulverton. As for the Culm Valley Light Railway, threading a remote valley of the Blackdown Hills a good 15 miles south east of Exmoor, the only justification for its inclusion here is its neatness and calm solitude, which aptly fit the atmosphere of the Fair Moor.

14 The Ilfracombe Branch

Length: 15 miles
Opened: 1874
Closed: 1970
OS: 1:50,000 map 118

By 1870 Ilfracombe was a growing seaside resort, and casting longing eyes in the direction of the railhead at Barnstaple. Supporters of two proposed schemes for lines across the hills took part in street riots before the more westerly of the routes finally opened in 1874.

From Barnstaple Junction station the line crossed the River Taw on a bridge 'of surpassing ugliness' (now demolished) and ran into Barnstaple Town station (555333), which totters into decay on its platform. Beyond the station there is a fine view from the track of Barnstaple sprawling along the banks of the Taw estuary. The line runs on a narrow shelf between flat marshy fields and the muddy foreshore of the estuary, past the castellated frontage of Heanton Court whose owner, Sir William Williams, bitterly opposed the railway which spoilt his view. One wonders what he would think of the discos that rock his stately pile nowadays.

The walker passes the RAF base at Chivenor and the restored station at Wrafton before reaching scruffy, forlorn Braunton station with its wooden shelter and signal box.

From here the track begins to climb, at first gently up the winding, narrow Caen Valley among plantations of conifers where ravens and buzzards are often seen. Then a 100:41

gradient post marks the start of a tremendous struggle up the flank of the hills into open moorland, with wide views of the sea at the summit where Mortehoe & Woolacombe station perches in the teeth of the frequent gales. The railway dips abruptly downhill through deep, rocky cuttings (another gradient marker shows 1320:68) and threads the twin bores of the dripping $69\frac{1}{2}$yd tunnel above the Slade reservoirs. The *Ilfracombe Chronicle* of 1 August 1874 recorded the reactions of a yokel on seeing his first train here:

> '. . . her puffed and blowed and come on an' on till her
> got nearly close up to where I waz standin' and then
> all at once when un zeed me her waz vrightened and
> bolted into a hole i' th' wall.'

The branch continues to wind down the hillside, with views ahead of the town and its surrounding cliffs, finally reaching Ilfracombe station site on an artificial plateau 225ft above sea level (514468). The buildings have gone, replaced by a modern office block, but the circle of the turntable can be seen; the sea winds used to take control and revolve the engines on the table unless a sleeper was wedged into the pit to stop them!

15 The Lynton & Barnstaple Railway

Length: $19\frac{1}{4}$ miles
Opened: 1898
Closed: 1935
OS: 1:50,000 map 180

The Lynton & Barnstaple, like the Somerset & Dorset, is one of those railways that has fixed itself forever in the affections of railway lovers and holiday makers. This long lived popularity can be attributed to the lovely, wild countryside that the little narrow-gauge line passed through, the diminutive rolling stock and tiny, hardworking engines, named *Yeo, Exe, Taw, Lew* and *Lyn* after local rivers, that rattled and chuffed so willingly up the long gradients, and the independent spirit of a company that somehow managed to survive isolation, poor passenger returns and harsh environment right up to the general grouping of 1923, when it fell exhausted into the waiting arms of the Southern Railway. To descend from a London & South Western Railway express in all its majesty at Barnstaple Town station, cross the platform and step into one of the L&B's crimson and white coaches was to enter a more leisurely world where for a full hour and a half you could enjoy the magnificent scenery along nearly 20 miles of winding moorland track.

The Lynton & Barnstaple track bed curves through 180 degrees out of the tumbledown Barnstaple Town station (555333) and passes the wharves by the river before running across Pilton Causeway into Pilton Yard, once the nerve centre of the L&B and now a goods store. You can pick up the track behind the British Legion club at the bottom of St George's Road, where it crosses the meandering River Yeo by broken bridges and climbs eastward among thistles and bracken towards Snapper Halt, sited on a long left-hand bend below the road. The tin hut and brick platform are half submerged in a muddy morass. A few hundred yards further on the railway crosses the Yeo at Collar Bridge and begins a 1 in 50 climb that continues for the next eight miles. The succeeding curves of the river shut off each valley in turn, and the L&B makes a series of right-angle bends to get through the hills, running in pinewoods whose thick carpet of needles and resinous scent make this a delightful section.

The eight arch Chelfham viaduct crosses the Stoke Rivers valley high above a school – the parapet has been removed for safety reasons – and great clotted lumps of lime, washed out by rain, adorn the piers. This is a good example of a viaduct lending drama and visual impact to an otherwise ordinary scene. Beyond the viaduct, the small station building is occupied, as is the detached stationmaster's house just below. The first stationmaster here, Mr J. Baker, had been the driver of the horsedrawn Lynton & Barnstaple coach before the opening of the railway put him out of business in 1898. Perhaps the fact that he had ten children to support persuaded the railway company to build him such a spacious residence.

The line passes through rhododendron woods where one embankment in particular vividly demonstrates the slope of the adjacent hillside – one side is 20ft high, the other 60ft. On the sharp curves at Chumhill, two railway workers lost their lives on 26 February 1913 when the ballast truck on which they were free-wheeling downhill skidded on wet leaves and overturned. The eight span steel viaduct over Lancey Brook is gone, but

Bratton Fleming station still stands as a private dwelling in a neat garden. The railway passes a series of farms mellifluously named — Southacott, Knightacott, Narracott, Sprecott and Hunnacott — and climbs steeply up through the woods to Wistlandpound Reservoir, a gunmetal sheet of water among low hills. At the top end the line swings round west and north, suddenly out on the exposed hilltop with views of Exmoor on the right, before arriving at Blackmoor Gate station, now the Old Station Inn, where the thirsty walker can drink a pint of draught bitter among L&B relics and electronic games where the tracks once ran.

From here the track falls away at 1 in 50 to Parracombe (Petrock's Combe), a little village of steep, narrow streets which boasts two churches. The older of these, the 11th century Church of St Petrock, was saved from demolition by a protest movement headed by John Ruskin. In the early years of the railway, Parracombe's rector, the Reverend J. F. Chanter, used to scatter seeds from the carriage windows along the embankments near the village, which still applaud his efforts each spring with a varied display of primulas. Parracombe Halt has a concrete shelter and a good crop of runner beans across the track, but Woody Bay station, two miles further on, is an altogether grander building in a curious pagoda style, nowadays shabby and neglected among its shelter trees. It served the resort of Woody Bay, three long downhill miles away, which never developed in spite of the pier it built in hopes of the tourists the railway would bring.

Foreland Point dominates the view ahead as the old railway passes Caffyn's Halt, built for the golfers who once alighted for a round or two on the nearby links. The line drops down Dean Steep beside and partly under the A39, and suddenly leaps up onto the hillside again for the final run in a private stretch of woodland into Lynton Station, 250ft above the town and 700 feet above sea level (717475). Lynton still remembers the black night of 15–16 August 1952 when the East and West Lyn Rivers, swollen by 30 hours of continuous rain, exploded down their narrow valleys and overwhelmed its twin town Lynmouth at the foot of the cliffs drowning 31 people. The isolation of Lynton

(*Opposite*) Chelfham viaduct (Lynton & Barnstaple Railway)

Blackmoor Gate station (Lynton & Barnstaple Railway)

station's position discouraged many potential passengers and contributed to the railway's closure 30 years before Beeching.

The present owner Bill Pryor hopes to open part of the line again; a Ruston diesel locomotive waits in his garden, and it is said that *Lew*, the only one of the Lynton line engines to escape the cutter's torch still lingers in South America where it went in 1935, although nobody among British enthusiasts has yet found it. One day Mr Pryor may vindicate the optimism of Paymaster Captain Woolf, RN (retd), of Woody Bay, whose wreath of bronze chrysanthemums at the closing ceremony in 1935 bore a black-edged card which stated simply:

'To Barnstaple & Lynton Railway, with regret and sorrow from a constant user and admirer. "Perchance it is not dead, but sleepeth." '

16 The Devon & Somerset Railway (Norton Fitzwarren to Barnstaple)

Length: 42¾ miles
Opened: 1873
Closed: 1966
OS: 1:50,000 maps 181 & 180

Leaving the Taunton to Exeter main line just outside Norton Fitzwarren, two miles west of Taunton (193255), the Devon & Somerset Railway sets out on its 43 mile run along the southern edge of Exmoor to Barnstaple. Shallow cuttings and flat fields lead to the site of Milverton station, the first of 13 on the branch, now buried under a new road that bypasses the village along the route of the old railway. The track soon diverges to the left, and swings round the hills that enclose the Saxon town of Wiveliscombe. The red brick station is used by a local builder and the cutting is blocked with rubbish, but beyond this point there is a clear walk through hilly farmland to the 447yd Bathealton tunnel, a black hole among bushes with a point of light at the further end. Waterrow viaduct, a lattice girder structure 162yd long and 101ft high, took the line over the River Tone; the girders are gone, but the great stone piers rise up out of the deep, wooded cleft like giant factory chimneys. A short stretch of the A361 brings the walker to Venn Cross station (666ft above sea level), now an isolated private house flanked on one side by the inky mouth of the 243yd tunnel and on the other by the stone goods shed. Here the line leaves Somerset for Devon. A good level path in rather dull fields leads to Morebath station, renamed 'Pixie's Laughter Cottages' – what would the stationmaster think? A mile further on, the Exe Valley line comes up from Bampton and trails in on the left to join the D&S just before Morebath Junction Halt, a crumbling concrete platform.

Now the railway runs in a cutting up to a broken bridge over the River Exe, where the Exe Valley Fishery stockpools are alive with leaping fish. Beyond the fishery stands Dulverton station – goods shed, stationmaster's house, signalbox, offices with cast iron canopy and platforms – all slowly rotting away below the beetle-browed Carnarvon Arms Hotel, a good two miles south of Dulverton itself. A tranquil green stretch of country follows; woods, marshy tracks, fields and hills all round. Nightcott tunnel is merely an elongated bridge, spangled with stalactites of lime. The line climbs steeply to its summit (700ft) at East Anstey, where the little orange and black stone station and goods shed are privately owned. Between rounded hills and scattered copses where buzzards wheel the Devon & Somerset continues on falling gradients past Yeo Mill Halt and Bishop's Nympton & Molland station, the latter a very smart house. It is well worth turning aside here to take the narrow lane up the hill to Molland, where the church is a gem – an unrestored Georgian remnant with box pews and leaning pillars – and the tiny moorland pub is equally unspoilt.

The line crosses the Yeo on an intact bridge and runs as straight as a ruler to South Molton station, a mile to the north of the old market town. Sheep trains crammed the sidings here when South Molton held its great sheep fairs, and rabbit specials went away between the wars until myxomatosis killed them off. The mud cones of swallows' nests line the eaves of the dignified two-storey building.

Soon the railway enters the wooded parkland of the Castle Hill estate through the 321yd Castle Hill tunnel, and stops abruptly at the towering piers of the viaduct that carried the line over the deep gorge cut by the River Bray on its way south to join the Taw. The great house on Castle Hill looks for all the world like a Georgian fantasy, but in fact it is a fairly recent reconstruction of the original mansion, built in 1684 by the Fortescue family, which was burnt down.

Filleigh station, regularly used by Henry Williamson, author of *Tarka the Otter*, has been maintained by its owner much as it was when the last train ran through; but Swimbridge, $3\frac{1}{2}$ miles further on, has vanished. The path, often of bridleway standard, continues into the outskirts of Barnstaple, passing the tall embankments that carried the loop line to the London & South Western Railway Barnstaple Junction station, and finishes at the Great Western Railway Victoria Road station (566327). The large stone goods shed still stands, and beyond it a tiny weighbridge office, but the passenger platform and buildings have been replaced by a car park.

17 The West Somerset Mineral Railway

Length: 11 miles
Opened: Comberow 1857; Gupworthy 1859
Closed: 1898
Reopened: Watchet to Brendon Hill 1907
Abandoned: 1910
OS: 1:50,000 map 181

The West Somerset Mineral Railway was built by the Brendon Hills Iron Ore Company to transport the ore from their mines 800ft up in the Brendon Hills to the harbour at Watchet.

Short lengths of rail are still embedded in the West Pier at Watchet harbour (071435), where the ore was loaded into ships and taken across the Bristol Channel to Newport and the great steel works of Ebbw Vale. The course of the line passes the 'Old Station House' and stone goods shed, and runs beside the track of the West Somerset Railway (the privately-operated local company which now runs part of the Taunton–Minehead branch) to Washford, where there is a private house on the site of the WSMR's station. An overgrown cutting and embankments take the mineral railway southwards past the ruins of Cleeve Abbey to Torre level crossing, where the tiny red stone crossing keeper's hut is dated 1871. Ore trucks packed with miners would hurtle through here on their way to Watchet, gravity their only motive power; they hitched onto the engines going back up to Brendon Hill for the return journey.

Ahead is a fine view of the steep slopes of the Brendons, cut into deep tree lined combes. At Clitsome another diminutive hut guards the road crossing, and Roadwater station has been converted to a house. For the next $1\frac{1}{2}$ miles the railway is a tarmac road, and after passing a row of cottages becomes a rough track to Comberow (pronounced 'Coombe Row'). From just

Comberow incline (West Somerset Mineral Railway)

south of the old stationmaster's house here, the great incline rises up at 1 in 4 through the woods. Passengers could travel up and down at their own risk. The full effect of the gradually converging parallel sides of the cutting is obscured by the trees, but as you struggle up the incline, whose rotting sleepers give a much needed toe-hold, you cannot fail to marvel at the faith invested by the company in such a massive piece of engineering. The view from the summit over Bridgwater Bay is quite superb. At the top, built into the embankment, is the winding house, partially restored by Mr Norman, the farmer who owns the incline and surrounding land. His house, just across the road, was once Davis's Stores which served the mining community at Brendon Hill. In his garden stands the immaculately maintained Brendon Hill station building, with a steeply pitched roof that extends over the platform as an awning.

The railway curves westward and runs along the gently snaking hogsback, through a series of farms and the site of Luxborough station, before terminating at lonely Gupworthy station, now a private house in a bleak and beautiful setting (965352).

18 The Exe Valley Railway

Length: 25 miles
Opened: Tiverton to Morebath Junction 1884; Tiverton to Stoke
        Canon 1885
Closed: 1963
OS: 1:50,000 maps 192 & 181

From the site of the disused Stoke Canon station on the Taunton to Exeter main line (935977), the Exe Valley branch line curves away at the start of its 25 mile run up the lovely river valley to the foothills of Exmoor. The line crosses the Exe at a broken bridge at Brampford Speke, where a 1912 Great Western Railway boundary marker sticks up out of the grass. It can be resumed at Fortescue Farm and followed on a well-ballasted path through Thorverton to another broken bridge just short of Up Exe. The station is occupied, and boasts a blue enamel GWR trespass notice and another in cast iron warning employees not to leave coal truck doors propped open at weighing machines.

The hills each side hem in the narrowing valley, along which the branch runs in a straight line to Burn Halt, where a rusty lamp adorns the platform. To the left a slender suspension bridge crosses a deep pool formed by the Exe, a favourite fishermen's haunt. The stretch of track beyond is frequented by bulls, but the A396 provides a detour at need to Bickleigh Bridge, a famous beauty spot where the River (Little) Dart (not its more famous namesake passing through Buckfast and Totnes to Dartmouth) meets the Exe below a cluster of thatched inns and houses and the Exe Valley Railway station, crumbling elegantly below the road. Nearby lived Bamfylde Moore Carew, an eccentric member of the local landowning family, who became King of the Gipsies in the early eighteenth century. From here three straight, flat miles in close proximity to the river lead to Tiverton, an old wool market town with castle ruins dating from 1106, where John Ridd, hero of *Lorna Doone*, went to school.

The Exe Valley line runs northward from Tiverton through Bolham Halt, above the main road and below the famous gardens at Knightshayes Court. Walking is easy and pleasant in the lush river meadows, above which the gnarled oaks of Bickleigh Wood hang on a long cliff face that follows the bend of the river. Cove station is occupied, and a carefully sculpted water garden makes a welcome contrast to the banging and clattering of the dusty quarry. The river bridge here has been retained for use by the stone lorries, but the next one is broken and the track becomes impassable as it approaches Bampton. The town's annual horsefair attracted dealers from all over the West Country in its heyday. The houses lie huddled up under the hills; the west wall of the church contains a touching memorial of 1776 to a child tragically killed:

'Bless my little iiiii
Here he lies
In a sad pickle
Kill'd by icicle.'

From the station site and blocked cutting, the Exe Valley line forges northwards through the wood, past the crossing keeper's cottage at Lodfin level crossing, and swings round to the right to join the broad track of the Devon & Somerset Railway from Taunton to Barnstaple at Morebath Junction Halt (953246).

19 The Culm Valley Light Railway

Length: 7¼ miles
Opened: 1876
Closed: 1975
OS: 1:50,000 maps 181 & 192

The valley of the River Culm winds peacefully in a remote crevice of the Blackdown Hills. Its railway winds with it, the archetypal country branch, joining the three charmingly named villages of Hemyock, Culmstock and Uffculme with the tatty old station at Tiverton Junction.

Hemyock village square boasts a superbly over-decorated cast iron pump whose inscription celebrates at one blow the reign of Queen Victoria, the accession of Edward VII and the end of the Boer War. The branch runs from the one-time huge and busy milk depot by the river (138140), its ballast only now beginning to sprout grass, ragwort and the large umbrella leaves of giant hogweed. Here is an aspect of the valley which can only be enjoyed from the sharply curving old railway — glimpses of gurgling stretches of river, hidden farms, stalking herons and patches of yellow flags by the water.

At Whitehall Halt a thoughtful resident has painted a short history of the branch along his fencing rail. The line was built in

Bridge over the River Culm (Culm Valley Light Railway)

hopes of tourist traffic to the Wellington monument three miles north of Hemyock, but the Culm Valley Light Railway Company was always in difficulty. Locally recruited navvies abandoned the half finished works for the harvest fields, and the Great Western Railway worked it from the outset. All the river bridges are still there, and the firm ballast gives a good walking surface.

Culmstock station platform, level crossing gates and platelayer's cabin (with a fine collection of spiders' webs in the roof) are still there. The square-towered church dominates the grey roofed houses of the village where R. D. Blackmore once lived. The friendly Culm Valley Inn next to the station serves hot home-cooked meals. Just past the farm of Southey Barton are three Great Western Railway boundary markers stamped 1880, growing like iron toadstools in a lineside field.

Uffculme station, a bare patch of tarmac and buddleia bushes, is followed by a fine girder bridge over the river. Then the track passes Coldharbour Halt and lovely old Selgar's Mill (beware of the dog!) and threads a deep cutting below the A38 before coming to a full stop at the M5 motorway (035115), just before shabby, peeling Tiverton Junction.

The walk can be continued on the other side of the Junction along the 4¾ mile Tiverton branch, opened in 1848 and closed in 1967. Much of this little line has been ploughed up and returned to the fields. At Halberton, near the site of a once busy halt, the line passes under the Grand Western Canal by a two arch brick bridge. On the outskirts of Tiverton it joins the track of the Exe Valley line (see page 58).

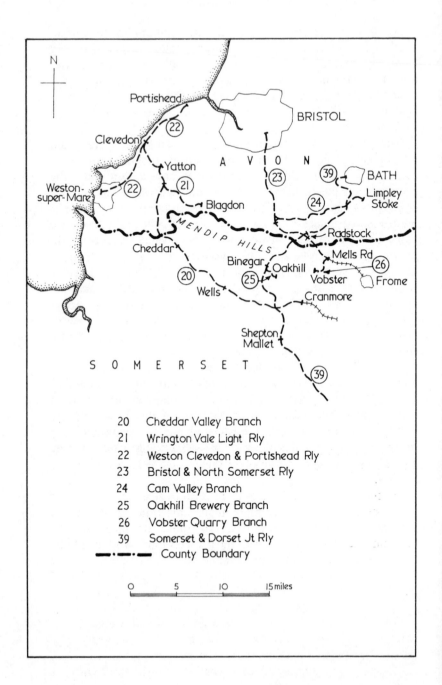

N

Portishead

BRISTOL

22

Clevedon

A   V   O   N

Yatton

39   BATH

23

21

Limpley
Stoke

Weston-
super-Mare

22

24

Blagdon

MENDIP HILLS

Radstock

Cheddar

Mells Rd

Binegar

Oakhill

26

20

25

Vobster

Frome

Wells

Cranmore

Shepton
Mallet

S   O   M   E   R   S   E   T

39

20	Cheddar Valley Branch
21	Wrington Vale Light Rly
22	Weston Clevedon & Portishead Rly
23	Bristol & North Somerset Rly
24	Cam Valley Branch
25	Oakhill Brewery Branch
26	Vobster Quarry Branch
39	Somerset & Dorset Jt Rly
—·—·—	County Boundary

O   5   10   15 miles

4

THE MENDIP RANGE

The main bulk of the Mendip Hills lies in a compact
whaleback of limestone across the neck of north Somerset,
barring the way south from Bath and Bristol. Under the heavy
blanket of drizzle or mist that they so often wear, the Mendips
seem a formidable obstacle, solid and grim. But this impression is
founded on outward appearances alone, for in truth the great
barrier is nothing but a tissue of water-raddled rock,
honeycombed by underground passages and caverns. Cheddar
Gorge and Burrington Combe, together with the spectacular
caves at Wookey Hole, present the most dramatic evidence of the
infinitely slow but drastic effect of running water on limestone,
which is in time eaten away into the caves, gorges and caverns so
typical of Mendip. Some of these underground features have
been explored, and a few opened up to the general public; but
vast numbers remain unknown beneath the lonely hilltops.

The Mendip range extends eastward from the M5 motorway
for about 25 miles. At its widest point it is no more than 10 miles
across, at its highest only 1068ft; physically it is a fairly
insignificant upthrust at the top end of the West Country. But
the Mendips have their own independent character – some
would say a bleak and desolate one – and a long and active
history.

On the north the land rises from Bath to Bristol in a series of
gentle swells up to the summit plateau. This upland plain, which
affords remarkable views over 50 miles or more of the
surrounding countryside, was mostly common land until the
middle of the eighteenth century, a great sheep run broken only
by the settlements of the miners of Mendip. Rich deposits of
minerals – lead, silver, iron and zinc among others – were mined
here by the Romans and their successors until the 1800s. A ring
of villages encircles the almost uninhabited top of Mendip, over
which clouds are always hovering ready to discharge their
contents. On a cold and windy day the Mendip plateau can seem
the loneliest and bleakest place on earth – then the sun comes out

and suddenly five counties are bathed in sunshine below you. In early medieval times the top of Mendip was another of the Royal Forests, and several kings stayed at the small and ancient town of Axbridge on the south side of the range to enjoy the hunting on the open heights.

Sheep made the fortune of many Mendip men, who left as their legacy the tall, graceful towers of their village churches; Chewton Mendip, Wrington and Leigh-upon-Mendip are especially fine examples. Shepton Mallet derives its name from the animals that created it, and the isolated village of Priddy, the only place of any size on top of Mendip, maintains to this day a thatched stack of hurdles on its green to mark the site of the annual sheep fair, still very much the main event of the year.

On the south side of Mendip the ground drops away in a steep escarpment where roads, lanes, and streams tumble precipitously down onto the wide expanse of the Somerset Levels. The full effect of this escarpment can best be appreciated from the Iron Age hill fort at Maesbury Ring, where a walk round the ramparts discloses views over the Levels from Dorset right round to Exmoor. Beneath the escarpment a string of south facing towns and villages shelter and bask in the sunshine. Strawberries and other soft fruit are grown here between Cheddar and Wells.

Mineral mining, paper making, and brewing were other important Mendip industries, along with coal. Much of the hilltop scenery on the north of the range is scarred by old slag heaps from the now defunct North Somerset coalfield round Radstock, but far worse rape of the landscape is being carried out by the quarry companies whose giant machines are nibbling away at the conglomerate limestone of Mendip and leaving their ugly gashes behind. Nor does the stone go to make buildings or bridges – it is crushed into tiny chips and tarred onto the roads. The quarrying concerns are now keen to rehabilitate the landscape as quarries become worked out, but nothing can undo the damage already done.

The Mendip Hills are full of history – the Iron Age barrows and hill forts, Roman lead workings like those at Charterhouse, the old Somerset Coal Canal in the Cam Valley, the mines of Radstock, the Benedictine monastery, abbey and school of Downside, and the remarkable west face of Wells Cathedral. Across the lonely hill top, up the flanks and around the fringes of

Mendip wind the railways that once helped to open up the range. The Cheddar Valley Railway, that undulated under the southern escarpment among the sunny strawberry fields (it was known as the 'Strawberry Line'); the Wrington Vale Light Railway that transported materials for the building of Blagdon Reservoir; the Bristol & North Somerset line from Frome through Radstock to Bristol; the Cam Valley branch among slag heaps and wonderful scenery; the little mineral lines that served breweries and quarries; and the railway that was synonymous with Mendip, the much loved and much missed Somerset & Dorset. All are gone now, except the line from Radstock to Frome which still moves large quantities of road stone. But from their abandoned track beds the walker can see for himself the great variety, the beauty and the bare loneliness of Mendip.

20 The Cheddar Valley Railway

Length: 31 miles
Opened: Witham Friary to Shepton Mallet 1858; Shepton Mallet to
    Wells 1862; Yatton to Cheddar 1869; Cheddar to Wells 1870
Closed: Passengers 1963; Freight 1964
OS: 1:50,000 maps 183 & 182

The 'Strawberry Line' offers an extremely varied and interesting walk in two distinct types of country, starting in the hills of Mendip and finishing across the Somerset Levels. Rocky cuttings and wooded valleys characterise the eastern section, *western?* while in the flat lands to the west tall church towers and ancient *east?* hill forts catch the eye.

From the junction at Witham Friary on the Westbury to Castle Cary West of England main line the route to Merehead Quarry is still used by stone trains, and at Cranmore station (667430), where wild life artist and steam locomotive enthusiast David Shepherd has built a splendid brick engine shed to house his collection of steam locomotives under the title of The East Somerset Railway, the track is also in use to Merryfield Lane, with an extension to Shepton Mallet in prospect. The Cheddar Valley line runs in cuttings and on tall embankments into Shepton Mallet, passing over the Somerset & Dorset Railway near Bullimore Farm. The Great Western Railway High Street station offices and shed of creamy stone are used as commercial premises. Here on 5 November 1858 'a prodigious multitude awaited the arrival of the first train with a band of music when old *Homer* arrived with the directors, decked with flowers from stem to stern.'

Falling gradients lead the line westward through steeply sloping farmland, with the view of the Mendips to the north often shut off by sheer-sided cuttings. At Dulcote Hill sidings trail off to a huge quarry, greening over at its eastern end but white and ravaged on the west. From Dulcote village to Wells is a straight run; the relief road for the overcrowded streets of Wells may soon be built along this section.

Up to this point the walk has been along the line of the original East Somerset Railway, whose station (built in 1862) stood just to the east of the level crossing over the Glastonbury Road. The grey stone building on the other side is the terminus of the Somerset & Dorset Railway branch from Glastonbury (see page 79), the first railway to reach the town in 1859. A few hundred yards further on is the Tucker Street station of the Bristol & Exeter Railway, which reached Wells from Yatton in 1870. Thus Wells was served by three railway systems – now it has none.

Leaving the towers of Wells cathedral behind, the Cheddar Valley line runs north west between strawberry fields under the flanks of the Mendips, through the stations at Wookey (a mile from the caves at Wookey Hole), Lodge Hill and Draycott. Wookey is a vehicle repair yard, and Lodge Hill, just below the village of Westbury-sub-Mendip, is Bristol Grammar School's Field Centre. Approaching Cheddar there is a spectacular view of the dark cleft of the gorge topped by the enormous scar of Batts Combe Quarry. Cheddar station with its twin gables and decorative barge-boards is a fine example of the Bristol & Exeter's style of building.

The branch rises at 1 in 100 to Axbridge station, now a youth club at the side of the ancient town's new bypass. There is a panoramic view of the Mendips, Glastonbury Tor, Brent Knoll and the Quantocks. Then comes the 180yd Shute Shelve tunnel. Thick deposits of lime have washed down through the limestone rock and collected on the tunnel roof, which is partly lined with brick but partly left with natural rock. Back in 1879, a gang of boys from the nearby Quaker school of Sidcot fixed a parcel of explosive chemicals to the rails in the tunnel for a prank. It exploded under the wheels of a passenger train whose driver had to pull up in a hurry, causing consternation in the carriages. The culprits were paraded in front of a GWR representative, who administered a stern lecture.

A cutting full of ferns leads to the commuter village of Winscombe. The station has been flattened, but a variety of fossils can be seen in the limestone foundations. The line passes Sandford Quarry and Sandford & Banwell station, now business premises, before striking out northwards across the flat moor. The hill fort on Dolebury Warren stands out to the east, another earthwork above Banwell to the west, while ahead is the hummock of Cadbury Camp with its Iron Age ramparts. The Leaning Tower of Puxton rises to the north west as the old railway runs on an embankment, past the junction with the Wrington Vale Light Railway (see below) and reaches Congresbury station (pronounced 'Coomsbury'). Tradition says that a yew in Congresbury churchyard was grown from St Congar's staff. It is supposed to flower at Christmas like the Glastonbury Thorn.

From Congresbury the Cheddar Valley Railway skirts the large village of Yatton and joins the Bristol to Taunton line (423659) at Yatton station. The walk can be continued from Yatton to Clevedon, another four miles.

The Cheddar Valley Railway Walk Society is negotiating the establishment of a path from Shute Shelve tunnel to Sandford, with possible extensions at each end to Axbridge and Yatton. Copies of the Society's booklet *Cheddar Valley Railway Walk – a Proposal* and a detailed list of the many plants and animals that have colonised the line can be obtained from the Secretary (address in Appendix B).

21 The Wrington Vale Light Railway

Length: 6½ miles
Opened: 1901
Closed: Passengers 1931; Goods (Wrington to Blagdon) 1950;
    (Congresbury to Wrington) 1963)
OS: 1:50,000 map 172

From its junction with the Cheddar Valley Line at Congresbury (432635) the Wrington Vale Light Railway runs south east for a few hundred yards, then swings due east for two

Blagdon station from the buffer-stops (Wrington Vale Light Railway)

ruler-straight miles to Wrington. The bridge over the Yeo is broken — you may be able to get across by way of the tree trunks in the river!

Wrington station is a coal merchant's yard. A red brick weighbridge hut and corrugated iron parcels shed still stand, and the arts and crafts shop on the other side of the level crossing calls itself 'The Signal Box'.

The track curves again through 90 degrees, crosses two arms of the Yeo by intact bridges and reaches Langford station on an embankment. Beyond the platform, one massive level crossing gate has almost become part of the hedge; there is some intricate iron work on the bracing bracket. Now the line has been absorbed by farmers into the fields — it emerges at Burrington to run in a shallow cutting below the grey stone stationmaster's house before diving again below the grass. The tall tower of Blagdon church is seen to the right as the old railway nears Blagdon station (503596), set in pine trees on the western end of the reservoir. The wood and brick building has been carefully restored and a square modern house built behind with stone blocks rescued from the demolished Worle Junction on the main Bristol to Taunton line. The owner has preserved the original lamps with 'Blagdon' printed in their glass, and some Great Western Railway signs and other railway relics.

Sign and lamp at Blagdon station (Wrington Vale Light Railway)

22 The Weston, Clevedon & Portishead Railway

Length: 14½ miles
Opened: Weston to Clevedon 1897; Clevedon to Portishead 1907
Closed: 1940
OS: 1:50,000 maps 182 & 172

The Weston, Clevedon & Portishead Light Railway rattled its way along the windswept coastal meadows from Weston-super-Mare to Clevedon and thence up the beautiful valley to Portishead. Heavily in debt and losing passengers steadily, in a district where they were at any time hard to come by, the railway was a doomed venture long before 1911 when Colonel H. F. Stephens added it to his empire of light railways. Even the energetic Colonel, who cannibalised one line to feed the next and handed out cigars to deserving staff, could not make the WC&P pay; and the second world war put an end to it.

From the railway's Weston terminus, a narrow area between houses at the junction of Milton Road and Ashcombe Road (328617), the path leads eastwards towards Worle before leaving the town and curving north east across the flat fields, a mile or so inland from the Bristol Channel. From Ebdon Lane to Wick St Lawrence it is used as a farm lane. The track runs past the station site north of the road and approaches the River Yeo. A short spur to Wick St Lawrence wharf (built in 1918) leads off to the left just before the river. The concrete and timber wharf itself, which once handled coal shipped from South Wales, now kneels half way down the river bank like a drunken dinosaur, slowly collapsing into the mud.

The Weston, Clevedon & Portishead Railway crossed the Yeo on a 240ft long bridge, of which only two pairs of slim iron legs still remain, rising from the slimy grey mud banks on each side of the water. The M5 bridge is the nearest crossing point – but the varied bird life of the tidal river should enliven your two mile detour. Four tiny halts and two river crossings further on is Clevedon station, the headquarters of the railway, where a red brick goods shed and a tall timber gallows with pulley wheel (for removing goods from wagons?) stand among bundles of waste paper.

From Clevedon the line runs a few yards to the right of the B3124 road, mostly on the level of the surrounding fields. At Cadbury Road station, the new houses built on the site are called Cadbury Halt. Note the pairs of concrete sleeper blocks on the track bed, interspersed by gaps for pairs of wooden sleepers – also some of the wooden sleepers themselves, supporting a few lengths of rusty rail.

The piers of the bridge over the River Yeo (Weston, Clevedon & Portishead Railway)

The track passes a loading bay in a field where stone from Black Rock Quarry's narrow gauge siding was transferred to the WC&PR and comes to How Ham Farm (469745) where it peters out among farms, playing fields and the complications of Portishead's outskirts.

23 The Bristol & North Somerset Railway

Length: 15 miles
Opened: 1873
Closed: Passengers 1959; Goods 1968
OS: 1:50,000 maps 183 & 172

A little-used mineral line runs up the valley from Frome to grim Radstock, pinched between its hills and slag heaps. Radstock grew rapidly in the late eighteenth and early nineteen centuries as pit after pit was opened up in the coal-rich hills. It was a rough, tough mining town – 'no Radstock girl need apply' was a phrase often added to Victorian advertisements for servants in the *Bath Chronicle*. Nowadays it crouches, bowed under the relics of its past and squeezed down in its narrow valley – ugly, but still tough and full of character. At Radstock the rails peter out, and the track of the B&NS wanders along the western edge of the North Somerset coalfield and reaches the heart of Bristol through its southernmost suburbs.

From Radstock West station (688549) the B&NS and the Somerset & Dorset's Mendip route keep close company for a few hundred yards; then the S&D's Five Arches bridge crosses the Bristol line and climbs away at 1 in 50 towards the top of Mendip. The B&NS line passes the site of Midsomer Norton & Welton station, less well known and much less attractive than its S&D counterpart a mile away. The branch runs through the fields past Farrington Gurney Halt and arrives at Hallatrow (medieval English – 'Holy Tree'), where the station building with its wooden canopy and iron pillars stands in the grounds of the stationmaster's house, a private dwelling. Beyond the station the GWR Cam Valley branch runs off to the right on a curved embankment, while the B&NS enters a long cutting which leads to the grassy platforms of Clutton station. The tree-covered hill on the right is actually the old slag heap of Clutton colliery, closed in 1921, whose ivy clad square brick chimney sticks up out of the side of the mound.

A succession of cuttings follows, at first in the woods and then half assimilated into the surrounding fields, each of which slopes at a different angle. A narrow overbridge stands right in the middle of a busy crossroads, causing chaos to the rush hour traffic. On the far side the B&NS approaches the flat-topped purple and brown hillock of Pensford Pit's slag heap, where there are extensive sidings and the remains of a rope operated incline to the top of the heap. The track crosses the 16 arch Pensford viaduct, 332yd long and 95ft high, with a striking view from the middle of the roofs of the village clustered round the stumpy tower of the church.

From Pensford station platforms the branch winds high above the tall grey stone tower of Publow church, crosses the A37 at a broken bridge with a 'Private – please keep out' notice, and runs over its summit below Maes Knoll to drop into Whitchurch, the first of a string of villages that merge into the conurbation of Bristol. An ugly, flooded stretch at the site of Whitchurch Halt is followed by a well surfaced path on a downward gradient of 1 in 60 – this is dog exercising territory, so watch your step! Ahead are the heaped up houses of the city on a series of hills. Gardens block the track, but a detour leads to a flattened stretch beside an ornate sports pavilion with an elaborate verandah near which Brislington station once stood. The path enters the grounds of Robertson's jam factory; then comes a final clear walk which terminates at a broken bridge and the buffer-stops of a siding (613718). From here rusty rails join the main Bath to Bristol line just short of the magnificent Gothic Temple Meads station.

This old railway, tackled from south to north as described in this section, brings the walker into Bristol from the countryside. But it makes an equally interesting walk the other way round, starting south of Robertson's factory, and travelling out of the city towards the hills.

24 The Cam Valley Branch

Length: 12 miles
Opened: Hallatrow to Camerton 1882; Camerton to Dunkerton Colliery 1907; Dunkerton Colliery to Limpley Stoke 1910
Closed: Passengers 1925; Goods (Hallatrow to Camerton) 1925; (Camerton to Limpley Stoke) 1951
OS: 1:50,000 map 172

In bits and pieces the Cam Valley branch was opened to provide an outlet for the coal pits strung out along the valley of the Cam brook. In bits and pieces it closed until silence returned to the mines, the railway and the old Somersetshire Coal Canal along which the branch was laid for much of its length. In 1953, two years after the last goods train wound its way down the valley, the Ealing Comedy film *The Titfield Thunderbolt* was made on the branch. Monkton Combe station was renamed Titfield and the ancient Liverpool & Manchester Railway 0-4-2 engine *Lion* (built in 1838) was pressed into service as the *Thunderbolt*.

Walking the branch today along the peaceful valley, only the slag heaps each side of the line stand as memorials to the thriving industry which once echoed among the overhanging woods. From Hallatrow on the Bristol & North Somerset's Radstock to Bristol line (633574) the slag heaps rear their flat heads over the sites of Paulton Halt and Radford & Timsbury Halt. At Camerton the Reverend John Skinner was rector from 1800 to 1839; he was a lonely man, an aesthete and classical philosopher in an environment of pits, pubs and pay night punch-ups, who poured out his sorrows in 98 meticulous volumes of a diary now in the British Museum. Camerton has done him less honour than its miners – the dramatic statue of a powerful collier stands in a pub forecourt beside the line. The closure of Camerton colliery in 1950 was the coup de grace for a branch already dead on its feet.

The route becomes hard to follow through Dunkerton, site of another large colliery, and Combe Hay. Portions of the track have been ploughed into the fields, and there are numerous fences and broken bridges, including the viaduct over the A367 where a great embankment slopes down to the road. Minor roads keep close company with the branch, however, and from these the walker can explore the derelict 67yd long Combe Hay tunnel (originally a canal tunnel through which the railway was laid) and the remarkable series of 27 crumbling locks along the hillside beyond Combe Hay where the canal bed leaves the old railway and makes a horseshoe curve known as the 'Bull's Nose', rising 154ft in little more than a mile.

Midford Halt is followed by the Somerset & Dorset Railway Midford viaduct, under which the overgrown Cam Valley branch runs to cross the Midford brook and arrive at Monkton

Combe station below the school. The Cam Valley's infrequent goods train was christened 'The Clank' by the schoolboys, and the name stuck fast for many years. Soon the branch becomes a path, and recrosses the brook just north of its junction with the Bath to Bradford on Avon line (783620).

25 The Oakhill Brewery Branch

Length: 2½ miles
Opened: 1904
Closed: 1921
OS: 1:50,000 map 183

Oakhill Brewery opened in the 1780s, and from its stone buildings in the village three miles north of Shepton Mallet the celebrated Oakhill Invalid Stout was soon pouring. Seven different beers were produced by the brewery, and after increasing demand had exhausted the delivery capabilities of horse and cart and a steam traction engine, the company built a 2ft 6in gauge railway across the fields to link up with the Somerset & Dorset Railway at Binegar station. Two tiny olive-green 0-4-0 saddle-tank engines, *Oakhill* and *Mendip*, puffed up the rising gradient from the brewery four or five times a day, hauling a train of flat wagons each of which carried 24 36-gallon barrels – and usually a contingent of local children on the downhill return trip! Harry Lambert, a local man who was an Oakhill Brewery engine driver, remembers winning a box of 50 cigarettes when the brewery manager bet him that he could not drive a load of 90 barrels to Binegar – 80 being the previous record.

The brewery buildings at Oakhill (634473) are in ruins, though Courage's Brewery still uses the maltings. The track of the railway climbs a steep slope behind the old stables, now a cottage mews, and turns right to cross three fields on a low embankment up to the A37 Shepton Mallet to Bristol road. The gap in the hedge between fields two and three is spanned by two rails, still in position. The Brewery branch crosses the main road on the level and turns right through a farmyard. It runs opposite the Mendip Inn, and then swings left down a shady lane, where sleeper bumps can be seen in the left-hand verge. At the bottom the trains turned right and chugged across two fields before crossing a minor road on a three-span steel girder viaduct. The embankment is thickly overgrown and bisected by a narrow broken bridge. Here I was lucky enough to find a stone screw bottle top inscribed 'The Oakhill Brewery Company' embedded in the earth.

The line threads a cutting between hedges and crosses a field below the S & D Railway, where a swathe of clinker and ballast is still turned up annually by the plough 60 years after the branch closed. The beer trains ran into their own stone-built unloading shed beside the main line (615492). Roofed with corrugated iron and still used as a store, it stands witness to the long departed Oakhill Brewery Branch.

Three years after the closure of its railway a great fire finished off the brewery itself, but the reputation of Oakhill Invalid Stout survives in the district. One man recalls how he bought his ailing and strictly teetotal grandmother a case of half a dozen bottles, with orders to drink a bottle with each meal. After a couple of weeks he visited her to find out how she was getting on. 'Well', said the old lady, 'I can't say I like it, but I've nearly finished the first bottle. I take a dessert spoon after every meal, just like you said!'

The brewery has recently been reopened under the title of the 'Beacon Brewery'.

26 The Vobster Quarry Mineral Line

Length: 2½ miles
Opened: 1857
Closed: 1966
OS: 1:50,000 map 183

At Upper Vobster Quarry the narrow gauge track of this mineral railway can be joined as it runs below the face of the workings (705496) and passes under a tall, narrow road bridge. Slightly embanked and clearly marked, the line curves from east to north and runs through a series of gates past Amey Roadstone's deep flooded quarry pits, as far as the rough road to Holwell Farm.

From this point the track has reverted to farmland, but a road runs parallel on the left, leading to the junction with the Frome to Bristol mineral line just west of the disused Mells Road station (712511).

N

Burnham-on-Sea
(27)
Edington
Jcn
(27)
Bridgwater
(28) Wells
(27)
Glastonbury
Shepton
Mallet
(39)
Evercreech
Jcn
Wincanton
Salisbury
Templecombe
Exeter
(39)

S O M E R S E T

TAUNTON
Langport
(30)
YEOVIL
(29)
Chard

D O R S E T

27   Evercreech Jc – Bridgwater – Burnham-on-Sea
28   Wells Branch
29   Chard – Taunton
30   Yeovil – Langport
39   Somerset & Dorset Jt Rly
━━━━●━━━●━━━   County Boundary

0   5   10   15 miles

5
THE GREAT PLAIN

If the Ancient Mariner had surveyed the Somerset Levels before the birth of Christ he would have felt at home. A vast lake of brackish, peat-stained water, tainted at frequent intervals by the encroaching sea, covered these 500 square miles of land, broken here and there by tiny islands. A wild race of primitive fishers and trappers of wild fowl poled their flat bottomed boats among the whistling acres of reed beds. They laid track-ways of wooden logs across the sodden peat bogs to help them keep dry from one isolated settlement to the next. At high tide the salt water surged unimpeded over the lakes and pools, bringing with it new game for the hunters and taking back to the sea the bodies of those who had ventured too boldly away from the safe places. Undisturbed by any outside influence, those hardy savages pursued their short and dangerous lives.

From Weston-super-Mare to Watchet the Somerset coast lies open to the sea. Behind the low sand bars which form the only natural defences, the highest points of land rise less than 20 feet and most of the Great Plain lies at or below sea level. Boxed in by the Mendips on the north, the Quantocks to the west and a curve of hills from south to east, this enormous tract of low lying country has always been vulnerable to high tides, and the problem is compounded by the number of rivers that attain sea level many miles inland. Until the monks arrived, the only parts which could be inhabited safely at all times were the knolls and hummocks of ground thrown up in the marshes when the surrounding hills were formed.

Ina, King of Wessex at the turn of the eighth century, had his stronghold at Somerton, where at least he and his men could keep their feet dry. When the Danes invaded Wessex, Ethelred was King; but it was left to his brother Alfred to rally a few desperate warriors at Ethandune (now Edington) in 787 AD and deal the interlopers such a blow that they were forced to seek peace terms. Alfred had their King, Guthrum, baptised at Wedmore to set the seal on the victory.

By now intrepid bands of monks were beginning to establish a presence in the water-logged fens, and with their customary zeal they devoted what energy they had left after building their magnificent abbeys to draining the marshes and making roads, fish ponds and fields. One wonders how many of the fisher folk came under the influence of the cross – even today the dwellers on the Levels are a notably independent people who keep their own counsel against outside pressures!

The enormous work of reclamation went steadily on until the sea was penned back behind the sand bars in Bridgwater Bay, only at exceptionally high tides to recapture its rightful domain. The rivers Brue and Parrett were confined to appointed channels – at least in dry weather. Rhynes and ditches carried the excess water from the fields to the rivers, whence it could empty harmlessly into the sea. Large scale agriculture became possible, and fisheries provided an important boost to the area's economy. Then in 1539 the Thunderbolt from Heaven swept away the monks and all their works. Many of their protective banks and drains fell into disrepair, and the lush pasture and arable land began to disappear again under the greedy water. A wet marsh country came into being. Only with the advent of the commercial peat companies a hundred years ago were the Levels once more brought properly under control The drainage ditches were repaired and increased in number, and the precious fuel was cut like black cheese from the drying land; 20th century economics have seen peat lose its status as a fuel, but it is still claimed from the Levels for use as a fertiliser. Withies were – and still are, though on a diminishing scale – grown around Sedgemoor to provide the raw materials for basket weaving.

Railways in this sparsely populated area are surprisingly thick on the ground, the principal one being Brunel's classic West of England line that arrows straight down the western flank of the flat lands from Bristol to Taunton, pausing only for a quick side-step in the direction of Weston. Bridgwater greeted it in 1841, Taunton a year later. The 1856 line from Frome to Yeovil neatly delineates the eastern extent of the Great Plain. Slicing it across the middle is the Great Western's new improved line to Taunton from Westbury, which gave travellers a respite from the GWR (Great Way Round) route to the far South West via Bristol when it was opened in 1906. These three railway routes still operate. But meandering across the marshes and low lying fields are five

railways of a different nature – splashy, sedgy tracks where
waterproof footwear is of more importance than the BR
timetable. The tranquil stretches of the old branch lines from
Chard to Taunton and from Yeovil to Langport may be dry
under foot if you are lucky – those that once served the placid
city of Wells and the historic town of Bridgwater probably won't
be. The Somerset & Dorset's branch, marshiest of all, that leaves
the southernmost outliers of the Mendips for the Vale of Avalon
and the seaward lip of the Great Plain, has on occasions seen
such flooding that the trains appeared to be floating in a sea of
spray. Walking here, from Arthur's isle towards Bridgwater
Bay, the railway rambler is surrounded by the ghosts of ancient
battles: Alfred's hunted army defying the Danish hordes, and the
disorganised rabble of the Duke of Monmouth's band of
peasants that in 1685, in the last battle fought on English
ground, foundered among the sodden rhynes of Sedgemoor and
left its pickings for Bloody Judge Jeffreys.

27 A Somerset & Dorset Branch

Length: 24 miles
Opened: Highbridge to Glastonbury 1854; Highbridge to Burnham-
on-Sea 1858; Glastonbury to Evercreech 1862
Closed: Passengers (Highbridge to Burnham-on-Sea) 1951;
(Evercreech to Highbridge) 1966; Goods (Highbridge to
Burnham-on-Sea) 1963
OS: 1:50,000 maps 183, 182

On any summer Saturday in the 1950s the tiny Somerset
village of Evercreech could be sure of an influx of railway
enthusiasts, cameras and notebooks at the ready. At Evercreech
Junction, a mile and a half to the south of the village, steam
engines snorted and shunted all day long, piling up in reeking
lines in the centre of the tracks, gulping water at the pipes or
standing at the signals whistling for the 'off'. Heavy expresses
loaded with holidaymakers had to be assisted over the Mendip
Hills, and Evercreech Junction was the marshalling point for the
bankers. Everyone stopped at the Junction – but it was often a
prolonged stop for those travellers destined for the old fashioned
coaches and obsolete locomotives of 'The Branch'.

The original main line of the Somerset Central Railway runs
for 24 miles across the flat peat moors of the Somerset Levels, a

dead straight line (except for a wriggle around the hummock of Glastonbury) from Evercreech to the decaying holiday resort of Burnham-on-Sea on the Parrett Estuary. After the Somerset & Dorset Joint Railway Company completed its Bath extension from Evercreech in 1874, the Mendip route became its main line, and the track across the Levels was relegated to the status of a branch. 'Going from nowhere to nowhere over a turf moor' was a contemptuous description of the Somerset Central at its 1854 opening, and nowadays the traveller on foot over the route penetrates a countryside secretive, isolated and with an atmosphere quite unlike any other part of the West Country.

At Evercreech Junction (636371) the track of the S&D main line from Bath swings into the station on a very tight south-easterly bend; but the branch strikes out straight and level towards Pylle Station, situated on the far side of the Fosse Way (A39), just below road level. The stationmaster's house and goods shed occupy opposite ends of the same large building of grey Mendip stone, now a private house.

From the station the line drops down a long bank through Pylle Woods, running in a cutting with young trees growing on the track bed, and emerges above Pilton Park's neat grassland and stands of old oaks. These earthworks are the last link the branch has with the S&D's Mendip route; from here on the line is only slightly raised above the surrounding fields. Level crossings abound. Though their gates are gone, all the crossing keepers' cottages are occupied.

West Pennard station has become commercial premises, a good mile and a half from the village – no concessions in railway days to the country customers! Farmers have built cowsheds and pens across the track on Hearty Moor. Some of the gate catches are still stamped 'S&DJR'.

Glastonbury Tor with its crowning tower beckons the walker on along the line which runs under the A39 Wells Road and curves round the north west corner of Glastonbury, throwing off a branch of its own on the right-hand side in thick bushes; this is the 5½ mile line to Wells (see page 83).

Glastonbury is a place so surrounded by myth and magic that it would take a whole book to do it justice. Here are the enormous ruins of the Benedictine abbey which rose on the site of a church burnt down in 1184 – a towering building 594ft long, crossed by 175ft of transept, whose nave soared 100ft high. King Arthur's grave was discovered here in 1190. Glastonbury seems to have been a Christian centre from Roman times; Joseph of Arimathea and Jesus Himself are reputed to have come to the water-girt island in the marshes. The Glastonbury Thorn, grown from a splinter of the cross planted by Joseph, still flowers at Christmas. On the Tor the 60th and last Abbot, Richard Whiting, was hanged in 1539.

The Quaker family of Clark had been making shoes in the village of Street for some 20 years before the Somerset Central opened, and James Clark vigorously promoted the railway. But the line ran to Glastonbury and the station was built here. A tall brick house, 'The Pollards', overlooks the station; the offices of the whole Somerset & Dorset system were based in this unpretentious building until 1877. Glastonbury & Street station, built of wood, still stands rotting on its platform, the timber walls and awnings now a dirty grey.

The branch runs on, mile after mile of level track across the remote moors of the Somerset Levels. It is a flat, peaty land, the solid ramparts of the Mendips rearing up in the distance on the right, and nearer at hand on the left the low bank of the Polden Hills. Herons step disdainfully among the scummy craters of disused peat beds, and water glints in the long silver rulers of drainage channels known in their varying sizes as ditches, lakes, drains, rhynes and rivers. Rows of neatly stacked brown bricks of peat march away from the old railway; peat cutting is the main non-agricultural industry in the Levels. Stands of birch and beech are being cut down to claim the underlying peat, whose sharp acidic smell is in the nostrils from here to Highbridge. Drainage engines fill the air with their tinny clatter, and blue whisps of peat smoke and wood fires rise up on all sides. Substantial red brick houses stand at the end of lonely marsh roads, completely cut off from their neighbours.

The track runs over a dry canal bed and the river Brue and passes the site of Ashcott station. Just beyond the level crossing the line is traversed on the level by the narrow gauge (2ft) railway of the Eclipse Peat Company, whose diminutive petrol engined locomotives pull trains of wooden trucks between the peat beds and the works buildings. On a foggy August morning in 1949 one of these little trains stalled on the crossing, and was hit by the 8.05 am from Glastonbury. The engine crew jumped for their lives, but the engine itself, 3F 0-6-0 No 3260, left the rails and buried its nose in the South Drain beside the line. The shaky ground would not bear the weight of a crane, so the engine and tender had to be cut up piece by piece and removed from the drain, an operation which took eight days and much sweated labour by a demolition gang working up to their knees in mud and water.

The old railway becomes a road, firmly surfaced and used by Peat company vehicles. It passes the site of Shapwick station and reaches Edington Burtle station as a muddy lane beside the South Drain. Nowadays Edington Burtle is a private house. The 'Tom Mogg' pub has a sign depicting Tom, the porter-signalman for many years at the station, holding a Somerset Central Railway handbell. Edington Burtle was once the junction for another branch from the branch, the seven mile run to Bridgwater. This line makes a pleasant walk across the moors, embanked for the first mile, and in a partly filled-in cutting at Cossington where the station is now a house. Bawdrip Halt has gone, and King's Sedgemoor Drain and the M5 block the route. At Bridgwater the brick railway buildings still stand.

The Somerset Central forges on from Edington Burtle across the deserted moors and comes to a halt at a broken bridge over the Brue. The clanging desolation of the milk factory at Bason Bridge is hard to take after the solitary miles of moorland. Station platforms and level crossing gates are still there. Beyond the station the ballast is heavy and pale grey – a reminder that milk trains used this section of the branch until the M5 cut it off from Highbridge. An underpass goes below the motorway and comes out beside new factories. Once this area was covered by the echoing buildings and maze of railway tracks of the Somerset & Dorset's Locomotive, Carriage and Wagon Works, closed in 1930 but only recently demolished. From these sheds rolled out the carriages in their famous prussian blue paint, lined in gold, the official livery of the railway. Some crumbling lengths of concrete platform, just before the main West of England line, mark the Somerset & Dorset's Highbridge station. The main line is crossed by a nearby road bridge although the S&D and Bristol & Exeter lines crossed on the flat. Evercreech Junction to Highbridge survived until 7 March 1966, but Highbridge to Burnham had been closed three years earlier in 1963. The route can be followed by the ornamental lakes of the nearby holiday camp and through a featureless housing estate.

The end of the branch is marked by a long curving platform (303488), added to the original station to accommodate the excursion trains of a growing seaside resort. Burnham was a popular choice for Sunday School treats and Bank Holiday excursions in the 1950s and 1960s. Though regular passenger services from Highbridge were axed in 1951, excursion specials continued to call at the terminus for another 11 years.

Today the little resort is sinking back into peaceful obscurity again. With Weston-super-Mare's amusement arcades a quarter of an hour's drive away, few holiday makers prefer the mud flats and cold winds of the Parrett Estuary. The days are long gone when wagons, and perhaps carriages, were run on rails beyond the station on to the concrete length of Burnham Pier to connect with the S&D's own shipping fleet. But just across from the station site, the thirsty walker can reflect on his tramp across the Somerset Levels over a pint in the Somerset & Dorset Hotel.

28 The Wells Branch

Length: 5½ miles
Opened: 1859
Closed: 1951
OS: 1:50,000 map 182

This short walk is dominated by the high wall of the Mendip Hills, forming a dramatic backdrop to the towers of Wells Cathedral which lie ahead. The Wells branch can be picked up by joining the track of the Somerset & Dorset Railway's Burnham branch at the humpback A39 road bridge just north of Glastonbury, and walking westward for half a mile. The low embankment of the Wells line can be seen on your right, very overgrown, curving away northwards (501401). The railway crossing over the rhyne near Hartlake Bridge is still intact; then a straight, flat path through the fields becomes better defined as the railway reaches Polsham. Here the intermediate station on the line was built, in spite of the claims of the much larger and more lively village of Coxley a mile further north. The Wells branch was a byword for rural tranquillity and motionlessness; and looking at Polsham's large station house and the surrounding miles of quiet farmland, sparsely dotted with houses, you can appreciate why the little railway (an average of six passengers and ten goods trucks a day when it was closed in 1951) could not survive any serious financial reckoning.

At Coxley there are gardens and fences across the line; but once beyond the village there is a clear track, slightly embanked, into a housing estate on the outskirts of Wells. Just before this point the line passes a complex of gates from several fields converging on an erstwhile crossing; the rusted, pitted letters 'S.D.J.R.' are stamped into the gate hasps.

The branch bends round to cross the abandoned Great Western Railway's Cheddar Valley line and runs into the Somerset & Dorset's Priory Road station site at Wells, where an impressive grey stone building still stands (545452). Large and delicious walnuts can be gathered in season from a nearby tree.

29 Chard Junction to Taunton

Length: 15 miles
Opened: Chard Junction to Chard 1863; Taunton to Chard 1866
Closed: 1962
OS: 1:50,000 map 193

The local populace dancing, kissing in the ring and jumping in sacks; a pub full of navvies gorging hot beef and potatoes and washing them down with gallons of ale; a marquee full of gentry enjoying a select luncheon – what else but the opening of a railway? Thus on 8 May, 1863, the ancient town of Chard in the south west corner of Somerset welcomed the London & South Western Railway's three mile branch from Chard Junction (340048) on the main line from Salisbury to Exeter.

Chard was a cloth making centre that grew up around a broad central street. The Chard Canal linked it with Taunton in 1842; but after an active life of only 24 years during which the canal lost money the Bristol & Exeter Railway opened its own branch down from Taunton in 1866 and killed it stone dead. Traces of the old canal's earthworks that crawl like a family of millepedes across the map accompany the walk all the way to Taunton. John Stringfellow, a native of Chard, gave the town its other tenuous connection with transport history when he invented an aeroplane in 1847 driven by methylated spirits. Unfortunately the air turbulence blew out the burners every time the plane left the ground, and Chard had to yield second place to Kitty Hawk Sands and the Wright brothers.

The joint station at Chard was the scene of rivalry between the Bristol & Exeter and the London & South Western, each company having its own staff, signal boxes and sidings to the canal. The building still stands, now used by an oil company. North of the station site the line skirts round the Chard reservoir through a new industrial estate and housing development, Beechings Close, (no comment!), before emerging in fields and running on to disappear beneath a $\frac{3}{4}$ mile stretch of the A358. The bridges over the River Isle are still there, carrying the railway on a series of embankments and cuttings past the elongated village of Donyatt. The timber platform and waiting room hut of Donyatt Halt have gone.

Ilminster has maintained its character of a county town of the 19th century, a place of narrow streets and drapers' shops with elaborate wooden frontages. Ilminster station, a squat red brick building with a steeply pitched roof and tall chimneys which is now a house, is situated a good mile from the town centre. To the right is the grey bulk of the Horlicks factory, surrounded by fields in which scores of tethered bulls lie dopily awaiting the AI extraction man and his little black bag.

The old canal bed runs off to pass through an MOD airfield, and the railway track bends round the western edge in thick woodland past the site of Ilton Halt (opened like Donyatt in 1928 to woo a few passengers away from the roads) and Speke's Wood level crossing keeper's cottage, a rather more impressive building than the stations themselves.

A three mile stretch of featureless but pleasant grazing country, dotted with woods and farms, leads into a deep cutting at Hatch Beauchamp. The red brick station buildings, including a fine goods shed with double round-arched doors, have been taken over by a building firm, and the 154yd Hatch Tunnel is blocked. On the other side an embankment smothered in tall trees and undergrowth crosses the A358 by a broken bridge on the slant, and gives another three miles of easy walking on a 1 in 80 falling gradient.

At Thornfalcon (274237) the wooden station building lies below the dual carriageway main road, and on the far side the branch has been built over at Creech St Michael as far as its junction with the main line just outside Taunton. The view ahead is a fine one, with Taunton spread out at the feet of the Quantock Hills.

30 The Yeovil to Langport Branch

Length: 13 miles
Opened: 1853
Closed: 1964
OS: 1:50,000 maps 183, 193

The Langport branch runs out to the west from the site of Yeovil Town station (551154), much dug about and impassable where it traverses the perimeter of Yeovil airfield and the Westland helicopter works. A tramp across wet meadows brings the walker on to the line by a humped road bridge from where it curves through a damp cutting. The steep miniature mountain of Montacute ('mont aigu') gives a welcome touch of character to the walk, which passes the station site through a thick belt of woodland below the village.

Wellham's Mill is a tall old building just to the left of the track, which crosses the A303 Fosse Way at a broken bridge and runs between young trees into a new housing estate on the outskirts of Martock. This typical Somerset flatland village, strung out along two miles of road, has some fine large houses made of golden blocks of stone from nearby Ham Hill. The branch leaves the housing estate by its old level crossing over the B3165 and passes the station site, a wide wasteland presided over by the square solidity of the Railway Hotel. Hawthorn hedges form a rough boundary to the track as it runs straight across the moor – flat country threaded with sharply angled farm lanes and drained by numerous streams. Sheep are still grazed extensively here – and bulls!

On Thorney Moor, a mile past the site of Thorney & Kingsbury Halt, the branch line stops at a watery gap over the River Parrett. Until 1960 the Parrett burst its banks every winter and formed a vast lake around the ancient abbey buildings at Muchelney a mile away to the east. Flood defences were then erected in the shape of earth banks along the river. You can walk along the top of the flood wall to the road bridge before regaining the old railway and passing a rusting Great Western Railway notice threatening the goldfinches and woodpeckers with a 40 shilling fine or a month's imprisonment.

At Langport the branch line runs under the road bridge to trail round to the left and join the Westbury – Taunton main line in a cutting (408274).

THE EXCURSION COAST

The slice of the South Coast included in this section takes in almost all of Dorset, and to the west a long thin strip of East Devon through which the slender arm of the London & South Western Railway main line wriggles its way to Exeter, every now and then throwing off a branch to the coast. Dorset is a county of immense antiquity, having in the number of its pre-Christian earthworks much in common with Wiltshire, but feeling warmer and less remote than that great chalk-smothered plain. The geography of Dorset is divided into three latitudinal layers – a northern belt of highly productive farming and fruit growing country; the central spine of the Downs, which run at an average height of 500 to 600ft right across the county from north east to south west, pierced by its main river, the Stour; and a southern strip of wild heathland covered with heather and gorse and thick stands of pine-trees, the inspiration for Egdon Heath of Thomas Hardy's novels. Entering East Devon the distinct wall of the Downs becomes absorbed in a more general swelling of hills and deepening of valleys.

While the northern half of Dorset has preserved against the onslaughts of the modern age the green peacefulness so carefully recorded by Hardy, the south has fallen under the influence of two main predators – quarrymen and tourists. Just where the unique 10 mile spit of Chesil Beach rises to meet the mainland below Weymouth, the Isle of Portland sticks out like a miniature Gibraltar into the sea. Portland, like the Mendips, is a honeycomb, but a man-made one. Portland limestone was used by Sir Christopher Wren for rebuilding London after the Great Fire of 1666, and ever since then the great block of stone has been chipped away until the hideous scars of old and new quarries have completely covered it. Along the coast the Isle of Purbeck is made up of limestone, marble and china clay, each of which has spawned its own extraction industry and the attendant pits, holes and heaps.

Holidaymakers, too, have eaten away much of the solitude of

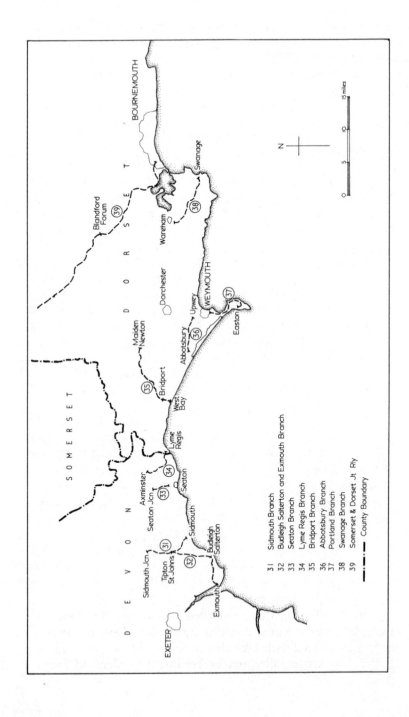

SOMERSET

DORSET

DEVON

EXETER

Exmouth

Budleigh
Salterton

Sidmouth

Tipton
St Johns

Sidmouth Jcn

Seaton Jcn

Axminster

Seaton

Lyme
Regis

West
Bay

Bridport

Maiden
Newton

Dorchester

Abbotsbury

Upwey

WEYMOUTH

Easton

Blandford
Forum

Wareham

Swanage

BOURNEMOUTH

31 — Sidmouth Branch
32 — Budleigh Salterton and Exmouth Branch
33 — Seaton Branch
34 — Lyme Regis Branch
35 — Bridport Branch
36 — Abbotsbury Branch
37 — Portland Branch
38 — Swanage Branch
39 — Somerset & Dorset Jt. Rly
— · — · — County Boundary

N

0   5   10   15 miles

Egdon Heath. Before any railways had penetrated this part of the world, Weymouth was an established seaside resort. It welcomed King George III's first public sea bathe with a spirited burst of music from a band concealed in a nearby bathing machine as the anointed head of 'Farmer George' broke the surface of Weymouth Bay. At first the town was rather stand-offish about the trains, though later, when the elders saw the enormous increase in trade that the railways were bringing to other towns, they changed their tune. Sidmouth and Exmouth in the west were likewise well established before the end of the Napoleonic wars.

The major development of the south coast of Dorset and East Devon, however, was intimately linked to three railway lines. A L. Castleman, a local solicitor, promoted a railway from Southampton via Ringwood to Dorchester known as 'Castleman's Corkscrew', which opened in 1847. Well south of the railway on the coast was an insignificant hamlet with a scatter of coast-guard houses and fishermen's cottages – Bournemouth. Within 30 years Bournemouth with its satellites Christchurch and Poole grew from nothing into a mighty conurbation, eventually getting its own railway direct from Brockenhurst joining the original line west of Poole. 'Castleman's Corkscrew' was extended in 1857 to Weymouth, on the same day and over the same rails as the Great Western Railway's line from Yeovil. These two railways were joined in 1860 by the London & South Western route from Salisbury to Exeter, which swept grandly across the whole county in a line north of the Downs, penetrated the hills at Crewkerne on the Somerset border and bored on through the Blackdown Hills to Exeter. Each of these three systems pushed out feeder branches to the villages and towns of the coast, in some cases merely supplementing an already thriving holiday business, in others breathing new and often raucous life into tiny settlements. The railway companies broke out in a rash of advertising, and a steady trickle of customers swelled to a flood in summertime. Some were on their annual holidays, but many were taking advantage of the cheap tickets offered by the railway companies – whole families on day excursions to the seaside. Roadside villages all over the area declined, and many of the traditional services associated with horsedrawn traffic (blacksmith, wagon builder, inn keeper) died out or became dependent on sparse local business. Channel packets began to ply between Weymouth and the Channel Islands, sponsored by the railways. Agricultural produce began to be moved by train, and local farmers and boarding house proprietors looked forward to a boom.

But the coastal resorts had been left fatally long without railway communication. In the cases of Budleigh Salterton and Lyme Regis the motorcar was about to burst on to the scene when they were finally put on the railway map. Long-distance passengers, bypassing the junctions and hurrying through to the big cities, were always the ultimate goal of the railway companies, and the little resorts were not helped by their lack of sandy beaches. Most had nothing but a sheet of pebbles between the cliffs and the sea, and had to rely for their attractions on 'magnificent coastal scenery' or 'fine cliff walks'. Soon the branch lines of Wessex felt the railway pinch; in time, one after another, they began to close.

Nowadays you can travel along part of 'Castleman's Corkscrew' and the Yeovil to Weymouth line by rail, although the original corkscrew between Brockenhurst and Poole no longer has trains. Trains still shuttle past the crumbling platforms and deserted car parks of Seaton Junction and Sidmouth Junction. But at Bridport and Budleigh Salterton, Lyme Regis and Portland, Abbotsbury, Seaton, Sidmouth and Swanage – here the roaring motorcar is king, and the old green tracks of the branch line railways wind silently up the river valleys from the Excursion Coast.

31 The Sidmouth Branch

Length: 8½ miles
Opened: 1874
Closed: 1967
OS: 1:50,000 map 192

From Sidmouth Junction station (now somewhat rebuilt and renamed Feniton), the track of the Southern Railway branch to 'Select Sidmouth' runs in a cutting (098991) for more than ½ mile before emerging close to the River Otter. As far as Tipton St John's the line follows the river down its lovely valley, a grassy path in meadows where sheep graze and herons fish along the

Just south of Tipton St John's, the track of the Sidmouth branch climbs at 1 in 45 into Harpford Woods on the left, while on the right the Exmouth branch runs beside the River Otter

banks. Ottery St Mary station is used as a youth club and Tipton as a private house. Just before Tipton the track crosses the river on a sturdy five arched brick viaduct.

At Tipton St John's the disused railway to Budleigh Salterton and Exmouth continues its level course by the river, while the Sidmouth branch becomes a rough road and climbs a long and steep incline (1 in 45) in cuttings lined with ferns, gorse, bracken and broom into the peace and beauty of Harpford Woods. There are some old and shapely stands of beech among the conifers, and the unexpected site of a French chateau, in yellow brick, complete with patterned slates on the steeply pitched roofs. This is Harpford House from which Lord Clinton, one of the directors of the London & South Western Railway, could see his investment hard at work.

At the summit the line becomes involved with recent road improvements — then a clear stretch leads down hill with wide views of the hills and valleys round Sidmouth.

The station (122885) was inconveniently sited 200ft above the town and $\frac{3}{4}$ mile from the centre, reputedly to discourage day trippers. It is a large and dignified building, in purple brick faced with yellow, its awnings supported by cast iron brackets whose design incorporates clover leaves and star shaped flowers. Several builders' merchants occupy the yards and goods shed.

32 The Budleigh Salterton and Exmouth Branch

Length: 11 miles
Opened: Budleigh Salterton 1897; Exmouth 1903
Closed: 1967
OS: 1:50,000 map 192

This branch can be followed from Tipton St John's (092917) as it runs down the Otter Valley between the bare platforms of Newton Poppleford station and over the Otter on an intact girder bridge. The white gatehouse arch and obelisk at Bicton — the Clinton Estate's popular gardens, show jumping and tourist attraction, with its own live narrow gauge steam railway — appear on the skyline to the right just before East Budleigh station (actually on the outskirts of Otterton), a rather heavy handed conversion to a house, though the platform flowerbeds are bright with shrubs.

The line climbs into Budleigh Salterton as a well used footpath provided with benches, passes the station platforms and leaves the town in a deep cutting between pine trees. Littleham station has disappeared, and new housing developments at Exmouth cut off the walk well short of the red brick viaduct that once carried the branch into Exmouth Station (000815).

33 The Seaton Branch

Length: (Colyton to Seaton Junction) 1¼ miles
Opened: 1868
Closed: 1966
OS: 1:50,000 map 192

Diminutive green electric trams now buzz northwards along the track of the Seaton branch from the old station site, near the little resort's sea-front, to Colyton, three miles inland. Colyton station is a red and yellow brick house on the edge of the pretty village that surrounds its church protectively.

From the tramway terminus (249944) the track of the Seaton branch runs through a farm where gates and cattle grids are made of old rails, and crosses a series of waterlogged fields with tall saplings growing in the ballast. Soon it diverges from the brook that winds away on the left, and joins the London & South Western Railway Salisbury to Exeter line at Seaton Junction, now closed and semi-derelict (248965). A concrete footbridge leads ghostly passengers to the Seaton platform, half buried in a line-side meadow.

34 The Lyme Regis Branch

Length: 7 miles
Opened: 1903
Closed: 1965
OS: 1:50,000 map 193

Until recently the cream and green painted wooden station at Lyme Regis (334924) still stood on a crumbling platform among Buddleia bushes high above the cliffs on Lyme Bay where the Duke of Monmouth first set foot on English soil in 1685 and where Mary Anning dug out her ichthyosaurus to turn the geological world upside down. The track of the branch to Axminster climbs steadily uphill in a deep cutting under flint bridges before running out on the hillside and crossing the nine arched Cannington Viaduct. The concrete used in this tall and slender structure was mixed with flints dug from the ensuing cutting, but the viaduct was always a shaky affair. Adams 4-4-2 tank engines were almost exclusively used on the Lyme Regis & Axminster Light Railway – they were the only locomotives light enough to cross the Cannington Viaduct and powerful enough to cope with the heavy gradients on the branch, although a GW 0-4-2T and LMR Class 2 2-6-2T were used right at the end.

Lyme Regis
Station

Combpyne Halt, set in a cutting in the hills, is privately owned, but a short detour takes the walker into the silence and solitude of the Combpyne woods. The leaf-strewn track skirts deep ravines where fallen trees sprout fern and fungus, and the banks beside the line are thick with bracken.

Soon the branch leaves the woods and runs in farmland, twisting and turning along the hillsides towards the scattered houses of Axminster. It crosses a bridge over the Salisbury to Exeter line and drops down an incline to its own grassy platform at Axminster station (292982). Thursday is a good day to do this walk as there are three markets in the town – and the pubs stay open all day.

(For a fuller account of this walk see *Walking Old Railways* by Christopher Somerville).

35 The Bridport and West Bay Branch

Length: 11 miles
Opened: Bridport 1857; West Bay 1884
Closed: West Bay 1930; Bridport 1975
OS: 1:50,000 maps 194, 193

This rural branch line, running through a little-frequented corner of Wessex, somehow managed to stave off closure until 1975. By then a single car diesel train was shuttling up and down the line, and local residents were loath to give up the convenience of their cars for the slow and bumpy ride through ancient woods and fields.

The Romans left traces of their civilisation throughout the countryside traversed by the Bridport branch. At Maiden Newton (595982) where it leaves the Yeovil to Dorchester line (itself a prime candidate for closure in the not too distant future), a mosaic pavement was unearthed, depicting Neptune battling sea monsters with a border of dogs chasing deer; and at Toller Porcorum, the first village down the branch, a stone carved with a ram's head is now the pedestal of the font in the Church of St Peter and St Andrew.

The line passes through the woods below Mount Pleasant and Hungry Hill, with the bare hump of Eggardon Hill (Hardy's 'Haggerdon Hill') on the left topped by a prehistoric fort and Roman ramparts. The cutting at Wytherston Farm is a haunt of dragonflies, the banks smothered in brambles and wild flowers. Beyond Powerstock station, a private house where the nameboards still stand, the branch runs down a wide valley on a long curving embankment between small knobbly hills. At Loders the guard had to get down from the train to open the level crossing gates beside the mill.

A few factory sheds by the line herald the approach to Bridport. The station was pulled down two years after closure – a shameful waste of a charming building in creamy hamstone with an enormous awning. Bridport has a long-established rope making industry – hanged men were once said to have been 'stabbed with a Bridport dagger.' Charles II, escaping to the continent disguised as a groom after the battle of Worcester, was recognised by an ostler in the yard of one of Bridport's inns, but talked his way out of trouble.

In 1884 the railway was extended another couple of miles southwards to West Bay in hopes of developing a resort to rival Bournemouth, but the boom never happened and the extension closed in 1930. Some of the track has disappeared under new roads at Bothenhampton, but from the three-arched bridge under the B3157 road a well marked footpath leads to the tiny West Bay station (465904), a boat builder's premises topped with a very steeply pitched roof and tall, ornate chimneys. The narrow-mouthed harbour is just beyond.

Toller Porcorum station (Bridport and West Bay branch)

36 The Abbotsbury Branch

Length: 6 miles
Opened: 1885
Closed: 1952
OS: 1:50,000 map 194

Over-optimistic hopes of extracting iron ore from an isolated valley led to the opening of the Abbotsbury branch in 1885. The mining plans came to nothing, and the line eked out its years as a purely local affair.

From the square grey station building at Upwey (667835), looking with its tall chimneys rather like West Bay station, the old railway runs westward through farmland, ploughed into the fields for much of its length. On the right rises the long line of the downs and on the left, hidden from view, is the pebbly strip of Chesil Beach. The wooden platform at Coryates Halt and the embankment beyond have been overwhelmed by brambles, but those who persevere will be rewarded by the sight of a Great Western Railway 'Notice is hereby given . . .' sign in the bushes and a boundary marker in a lineside ditch. Portesham station building and goods shed are privately owned. High on the downs above, a tall monument honours Nelson's friend Captain Hardy, who grew up in Portesham.

The 15th century St Catherine's Chapel on its knoll above Abbotsbury calls the walker on between conifers and grass meadows. The line passes stone-built engine and goods sheds and terminates at the neatly restored Abbotsbury station (582853). Of all the glories of Abbotsbury Abbey, founded in the 10th century, the chief survivors are the great 14th century wool barn – 276ft long and 31ft high – and the Swannery. The sub-tropical gardens on the beach road out of Abbotsbury with their peacocks and exotic plants are well worth a visit too.

37 The Portland Branch

Length: 7½ miles
Opened: Weymouth to Portland 1865; Easton to Portland 1902
Closed: Passengers 1952; Goods 1965
OS: 1:50,000 map 194

The Isle of Portland, a great block of freestone pitted and pocked with quarries, juts out into the Channel waters from the southernmost tip of Weymouth. Tucked into its northern shore is a large and busy naval base. Surmounted by a well hidden prison and a chilling mini-Dartmoor of a Borstal, nearly treeless, mercilessly carved about by centuries of stone working, battered by wind and wave, the island's rugged outlines prompted Thomas Hardy to style it the Gibraltar of Wessex.

The London & South Western Railway's title for Weymouth – 'the Naples of England' – is rather harder to understand. The dignified old seaside town where George III bathed to the music of the town band is the starting point for a walk along the old railway into the heart of the Isle of Portland. It took three railway companies – the Weymouth & Portland Railway, the Portland Breakwater or Admiralty Railway and the Easton & Church Hope Railway – nearly 40 years to complete the $7\frac{1}{2}$ miles of single track branch line.

Beside Weymouth's wooden station is the Portland branch's Melcombe Regis station building (678795), from which the branch crossed the Backwater, a sluggish arm of the sea, on a viaduct (now broken). A GWR driver once leaped from his engine into the water while crossing the viaduct, and was subsequently imprisoned for endangering the public by leaving his post.

A detour leads to the single curved platform of Westham Halt and the lofty Marsh embankment with a view over Weymouth to the Downs. The track continues as a well trodden path past the platforms of Rodwell station and the halts at Sandsfoot Castle and Wyke Regis, with a dramatic view of Portland's cliffs ahead, flanked by three great breakwaters.

The viaduct across the Fleet inlet has gone, but on the far side the track runs along the edge of Chesil Beach. The writer of an article in *The Railway Magazine* for September 1909 said of the pebbles on Chesil Beach: 'at Portland their size is that of a large potato, diminishing gradually to the size of a horse bean at Abbotsbury'. Chesil Beach is a unique formation, enclosing a specialised semi-marine world beneath the brackish waters of the West and East Fleet.

'Lo! Yonder to Portland's domains,
The steam propelled chariots come.
Receive the gay troops of the trains,
With banners, and trumpets, and drum!'

The Isle of Portland, with the branch line embankment running up to a watery gap where a viaduct spanned the Fleet inlet

Thus spoke the *Weymouth Telegram* of 19 October 1865, ten days after the opening of the Weymouth & Portland Railway. The track enters the forbidden territory of the naval dockyard below the forbidding ranks of the prison officers' quarters on the cliff face. By climbing the steep streets of Fortuneswell and then on upwards over the top of the island – with a wonderful view over the whole length of Chesil Beach – the branch can be rejoined on the eastern side after a dismal trek among rusty tin shacks and rubbish-filled disused quarries, past the prison and the gloomy, massive Borstal. The country's unwanted junk – human and material – has been brought here and dumped in this desolate landscape.

The line curves round through almost a complete circle in cuttings among more quarries to the terminus at Easton station, now vanished beneath new roads and barren ground, at the very centre of the island (691721). A few hundred yards to the north is the track of the Merchant's Railway, built as long ago as 1826, which carried stone down a steep incline to the harbour.

38 The Swanage Branch

Length: 10 miles
Opened: 1885
Closed: 1972
OS: 1:50,000 map 195

The Isle of Purbeck's branch railway runs south east for 10 miles from Worgret Junction on the Bournemouth to Dorchester main line, crossing a wide heath and squeezing through the Purbeck Hills at Corfe Castle. The first three miles from the junction as far as Furzebrook (934840) are used by British Rail as an oil wagon siding, but from here on there is an unobstructed path all the way to within ½ mile of Swanage. Gorse and bracken have spilled over from the surrounding heath on to the cutting sides, but the track-bed itself is perfectly clear – a rare delight.

At Corfe Castle the Corfe River has sliced a narrow gap in the chalky barrier of the Purbeck Hills, a gap neatly plugged by the great 11th or 12th century castle ruins on their hillock, dominating the little grey stone town at their feet. They have had a bloody history. Ethelred the Unready's mother, Elfrida, who lived here centuries before the castle was built, came to the throne by stabbing to death her stepson, King Edward the Martyr. Here King John starved 22 rebel knights to death. Edward II was imprisoned in the keep before his murder in Berkeley Castle. In the Civil War, the Bankes family repulsed one siege which featured 100 seamen from Poole with scaling ladders. Finally the castle was taken with the help of a traitor. Gunpowder had no effect on its stout walls and it was partly pulled down by physical labour.

Corfe Castle station stands below the ruins, a solid building of Purbeck stone with a fine canopy, a goods shed and some rusty signal posts. The branch runs on, following the southern face of the Downs, to the outskirts of Swanage. The rails of the Swanage Railway Society lead past a stone engine shed and turntable circle and wriggle between old carriages and locomotives to terminate at the large station building (029789). There are high hopes of starting a regular service from Swanage to meet British Rail passenger trains at a new platform at Furzebrook. Not all the local residents are happy to see trains running again on the branch, but the scheme is supported by local tradesmen and the Swanage Town Council. Boilersuited and woolly-hatted enthusiasts will gladly show you over their collection of steam engines, which includes a rare 0-6-0 tender locomotive built for colliery work by Peckett of Bristol.

In the course of its run from Worgret Junction, the Swanage branch crosses the tracks of three disused clay tramways, each of which can be followed on foot without much difficulty. Pike's

Corfe Castle station, with the castle ruins in the background (Swanage branch)

Tramway runs as a rough road due south from Ridge Wharf to join the branch at Furzebrook. The Middlebere Plateway crosses Middlebere Heath in a south westerly direction from Middlebere Farm, passing under the Swanage to Wareham Road (by two dated tunnels) and the railway branch at Norden to reach the clay pits there. Fayle's Tramway reached the branch just south of Norden after a $5\frac{1}{2}$ mile run from the Goathorn promontory by way of Newton Heath and Bushey. At Ridge, Middlebere and Goathorn the clay was transferred to ships, but these wharves are now long disused.

39 Serene and Delightful (The Somerset & Dorset Railway)

Length: $71\frac{1}{2}$ miles
Opened: Wimborne Junction to Blandford 1860; Evercreech to Templecombe 1862; Templecombe to Blandford 1863; Evercreech Junction to Bath 1874; Corfe Mullen Junction to Broadstone 1885
Closed: 1966
OS: 1:50,000 maps 172, 183, 194 & 195

It is fitting that this book should end with a description of the line which forms the whole of the eastern boundary of the territory I have taken to represent the West Country, and which runs through three of the six areas – the Mendip Range, the Great Plain and the Excursion Coast. It was a railway loved by photographers, steam enthusiasts and those who revelled in its beautiful scenery, and cursed by travellers on a tight time schedule. It wound its leisurely way from Bath over the Mendips and down the lush valley of the Stour to the sea at Bournemouth. Slow and Dirty or Serene and Delightful – the Somerset & Dorset.

The line starts at Bath Green Park station (745648), a neo-Georgian building backed by a magnificent cast iron train shed that has somehow escaped the demolition men since the closure of the S&D in 1966. Sainsbury's, the supermarket company, has bought it and hopes to restore it to its former splendour. The track leads away westward before swinging through 180 degrees and commencing a climb of 1 in 50 out of Bath. Steam engine crews regularly suffered near-suffocation in the narrow bore of Devonshire tunnel (now sealed off) before breathing in the fresh air of Lyncombe Vale, where a nature trail has been established on the line. The notorious Combe Down tunnel followed – over a mile of unventilated blackness.

On the far side of the tunnel, the track crosses Tucking Mill viaduct in Horsecombe Vale, and runs through the wooded fields south of Bath to Midford station, a single overgrown platform. The railway crosses the eight-arched Midford viaduct over four separate obstacles – the Bath to Frome road, the Cam Brook, the Somersetshire Coal Canal and the Cam Valley branch (see page 72) – and winds down the valley past Wellow station and Shoscombe & Single Hill Halt. The slag heaps of Radstock rise to greet the walker at the abandoned Writhlington Colliery buildings. Near here stood Foxcote signalbox, where the worst accident in the history of the Somerset & Dorset occurred on the night of 7 August, 1876. A series of errors led to a head-on collision between two crowded excursion trains in which 12 passengers and a guard were killed.

Radstock North station buildings, yard and engine shed have all been flattened, and the S&D leaves the ugly, tough little mining town side by side with the abandoned Bristol & North Somerset Frome to Bristol line before crossing over it at Five Arches bridge. Now the great climb over the limestone barrier of the Mendips begins: an uphill slog at 1 in 50 past Midsomer Norton (where roses from the signalman's garden still twine up his signal post), Chilcompton and Binegar stations for $7\frac{1}{2}$ miles, crossing from Avon into Somerset, snaking up to Masbury summit. Even the S&D Class 7F 2-8-0s, specially designed for the line, found this a gruelling struggle. Lesser engines often expired before reaching the top.

Masbury station looks out from its isolated perch over a memorable view of the Vale of Glastonbury and the distant Quantocks. The old railway dips downward for a 1 in 50 descent through the twin bore Winsor Hill tunnel, where a goods train was buried in a snow drift for three days during the blizzards of 1962/3. Hugging the hillside, it circles Shepton Mallet and crosses the long curve of the 27 arch Charlton viaduct into Charlton Road station, now a factory site. More falling gradients lead over Prestleigh viaduct to Evercreech Junction, a silent group of buildings where so much activity once took place. The S&D branch line to Burnham-on-Sea sets out across the moors on the right (see page 79).

Beyond the junction, to a gap where the S&D crossed over the GWR West of England main line, long straight stretches of track run through flat fields bordered by wooded hills – the craggy Mendips are left behind and Dorset lies ahead. Through Cole station where the Somerset Central and Dorset Central railways met in 1862 to form the Somerset & Dorset Joint Railway; through Wincanton, where milk lorries pound the streets day and night; through Templecombe, the scene of ludicrous manoeuvrings, shuntings, couplings and uncouplings as the S&D wrestled with the complexities of its relationship with the Salisbury to Exeter main line. Between Henstridge and Stalbridge stations the line, now a narrow single track path, crosses from Somerset into Dorset.

Sturminster Newton, approached in a deep cutting, is a lovely old town cradled by the winding River Stour which accompanies the S&D for the next 15 miles. Shillingstone station still sports its outsize canopy, erected in honour of King Edward VII's occasional visits, but Blandford station and a short viaduct here have gone without a trace. The Georgian town centre on its hilly streets is well worth exploring.

Charlton Marshall Halt, buried in its leafy cutting; Spetisbury, hard by the A350; Bailey Gate above the village of Sturminster Marshall – these stations are punctuation marks on the long straight line of the Somerset & Dorset as it runs through some of the loveliest and most unspoiled countryside on the whole walk. At Corfe Mullen the jungly track to Wimborne, closed in 1933, branches off to the left, but the S&D main line makes a great right hand curve through sand cuttings lined with gorse and heather beneath the pine trees after which the railway's famous holiday train 'The Pines Express' was named. It cuts through a golf course and drops down a 1 in 97 bank to Broadstone station on the outskirts of Poole.

Here the S&D's own track ends. The LSWR's Broadstone to Poole line can be followed as it falls to sea level, and trains still travel the route from Poole to Branksome. A mile to the east of Branksome station is a new development, a car park and buildings surrounded by elegant hotels (078914). Railway sleepers in nearby fences and a couple of green railway lamps jutting out from a wall tell the tale – this was Bournemouth West station, the seaside terminus of the Somerset & Dorset Railway at the end of its wanderings along the borders of the West Country.

(For a fuller account of this walk, see *Walking Old Railways* by Christopher Somerville.)

APPENDIX 1

A detailed examination of wildlife at one station site

One of the most striking features of the disused railways is the way in which they have provided refuge for hard-pressed nature. The uninformed layman can usually only guess at the variety of flora and fauna at any given site; but a number of places have been carefully surveyed by the Devon Trust for Nature Conservation. One station site has a special advantage over most other sites – fresh water is constantly flowing through the area from a moorland slope. The Devon Trust for Nature Conservation have requested that the site should not be specifically identified, partly in view of the possible effects on the habitat of an influx of visitors, and partly because negotiations are in progress for the sale and development of the old station.

The following lists give an indication of the importance of old railways to the regeneration of nature in an increasingly poisoned countryside – all these plants, animals and insects are crammed into an area of a few thousand square yards.

Plants

Achillea millefolium (Yarrow)
Aegopodium podagraria (Ground Elder)
Aira caryophyllea (Silvery Hair-grass)
Aira praecox (Early Hair-grass)
Alopecurus geniculatus (Marsh Fox-tail)
Angelica sylvestris (Angelica)
Anthoxanthum odoratum (Sweet Vernal-grass)
Armoracia (Radish)
Agrostis tenuis (Common Bent-grass)
Arabidopsis thaliana (Thale Cress)
Arctium minus (Lesser Burdock)
Arrhenatherum elatius (Oat-grass)
Asplenium trichomanes (Maidenhair Spleenwort)
Athyrium filix-femina (Lady-fern)
Bellis perennis (Daisy)
Betula pendula (Silver Birch)
Betula pubescens (Downy Birch)
Bromus mollis (Lop-grass)

Callitriche stagnalis (Water Star-wort)
Calluna vulgaris (Heather)
Calystegia sepium (Larger Bindweed)
Cardamine pratensis (Cuckoo-flower)
Carex echinata (Star Sedge)
Carex flacca (Carnation grass)
Carex ovalis (Oval Sedge)
Carex rostrata (Bottle Sedge)
Centaurea nigra (Black Knapweed)
Cerastium holosteoides (Common Mouse-ear Chickweed)
Chamaenerion angustifolium (Rosebay Willow-herb)
Chaenorrhinum minus (Small Toadflax)
Chelidonium majus (Greater Celandine)
Chrysanthemum leucanthemum (Moon-daisy)
Cirsium arvense (Creeping Thistle)
Cirsium palustre (Marsh Thistle)
Cirsium vulgare (Spear Thistle)
Convolvulus arvensis (Field Bindweed)
Crataegus monogyna (Hawthorn)
Crepis capillaris (Smooth Hawk's-beard)
Dactylorhiza praetermissa (Southern Marsh Orchid)
Digitalis purpurea (Foxglove)
Drosera rotundifolia (Sundew)
Epilobium adenocaulon (American Willow-herb)
Epilobium hirsutum (Great Willow-herb)
Epilobium montanum (Broad-leaved Willow-herb)
Epilobium obscurum (Short-fruited Willow-herb)
Epilobium palustre (Marsh Willow-herb)
Epilobium parviflorum (Lesser Hairy Willow-herb)
Eupatorium cannabinum (Hemp agrimony)
Euphrasia nemorosa (Eyebright)
Euphrasia officinalis (Eyebright)
Equisetum arvense (Common Horse-tail)
Eriophorum angustifolium (Common Cotton-grass)
Festuca rubra (Red Fescue)
Galium aparine (Common cleaver)
Galium palustre (Marsh Bedstraw)
Geranium dissectum (Cut-leaved Cranesbill)
Geranium robertianum (Herb Robert)
Glyceria declinata (Flote grass)
Gnaphalium uliginosum (Marsh Cudweed)
Hedera helix (Ivy)
Heracleum sphondylium (Hogweed)
Hesperis matronalis (Dame's Violet)

Hieracium pilosella (Mouse-ear Hawkweed)
Holcus lanatus (Yorkshire Fog)
Hypericum perforatum (Perforate St John's-wort)
Hypochaeris radicata (Common catsear)
Iris pseudacorus (Yellow Flag)
Jasione montana (Sheep's-bit)
Juncus acutus (Sharp Rush)
Juncus articulatus (Jointed Rush)
Juncus conglomeratus (Conglomerate Rush)
Juncus effusus (Soft Rush)
Juncus inflexus (Hard Rush)
Juncus tenuis (Heath Rush)
Juncus bufonius (Toad Rush)
Juncus bulbosus (Bulbous Rush)
Lapsana communis (Nipplewort)
Leontodon autumnalis (Autumnal Hawkbit)
Leontodon hispidus (Rough Hawkbit)
Ligustrum vulgare (Privet)
Linaria repens (Pale Toadflax)
Linaria vulgaris (Yellow Toadflax)
Linum catharticum (Purging Flax)
Lolium multiflorum (Rye-grass) – 2 sub-species
Lotus corniculatus (Birds Foot Trefoil)
Lotus pedunculatus (Ulisinosus) (Marsh Birds Foot Trefoil)
Luzula multiflora (Many-headed Woodrush)
Medicago lupulina (Black Medick)
Myosotis arvensis (Common forget-me-not)
Odontites verna (Red Rattle)
Ononis repens (Restharrow)
Osmunda regalis (Royal Fern)
Peplis portula (Water Purslane)
Pinus sylvestris (Scots Pine)
Plantago lanceolata (Ribwort)
Poa pratensis (Smooth-stalked Meadow-grass)
Polygonum cuspidatum (Black Bindweed)
Polypodium vulgare (Polypody)
Potamogeton polygonifolius (Pondweed)
Potentilla anserina (Silverweed)
Potentilla erecta (Common Tormentil)
Potentilla reptans (Creeping cinquefoil)
Prunella vulgaris (Self-heal)
Prunus spinosa (Blackthorn)
Pulicaria dysenterica (Fleabane)
Ranunculus acris (Meadow Buttercup)
Ranunculus flammula (Lesser Spearwort)

Ranunculus omiophyllus (Lenormand's Water-crowfoot)
Ranunculus repens (Creeping Buttercup)
Rhinanthus minor (Yellow-rattle)
Rosa arvensis (Field Rose)
Rosa canina (Dog Rose)
Rubus fruticosus (agg) (Blackberry)
Rumex acetosa (Sorrel)
Rumex acetosella (Sheep's Sorrel)
Rumex crispus (Curled Dock)
Rumex obtusifolius (Broad-leaved Dock)
Sagina apetala (Pearlwort)
Sagina procumbens (Pearlwort)
Salix aurita (Eared Sallow)
Salix caprea (Great Sallow)
Salix cinerea (Common Sallow)
Sambucus nigra (Elder)
Scrophularia nodosa (Figwort)
Sedum acre (Biting Stonecrop)
Senecio jacobaea (Ragwort)
Senecio sylvaticus (Wood Groundsel)
Silene dioica (Red Campion)
Sonchus arvensis (Field Milk-Thistle)
Sonchus asper (Spiny Milk-Thistle)
Sorbus aucuparia (Rowan)
Stachys palustris (Marsh Woundwort)
Stachys sylvatica (Hedge Woundwort)
Stellaria alsine (Bog Stitchwort)
Stellaria graminea (Lesser Stitchwort)
Stellaria media (Chickweed)
Tragopogon pratensis (Jack-go-to-bed-at-noon)
Trifolium dubium (Lesser Yellow Trefoil)
Trifolium pratense (Red Clover)
Trifolium repens (White Clover)
Tripleurospermum maritimum (Scentless Mayweed)
Trisetum flavescens (Yellow oat)
Tussilago farfara (Coltsfoot)
Typha angustifolia (Lesser Reedmace)
Typha latifolia (Great Reedmace)
Veronica arvensis (Wall Speedwell)
Veronica beccabunga (Brooklime)
Veronica serpyllifolia (Thyme-leaved Speedwell)
Vicia angustifolia (Common vetch)
Vicia sepium (Bush Vetch)
Vicia tetrasperma (Smooth Tare)
Viola riviniana (Common Violet)

Odonata (Dragonflies and damselflies)

All these species breed between the platforms, in an area no more than 150yd long by 40yd wide. The total of 18 species is only exceeded in all of Devon and Cornwall by one other site – Rackerhayes lake complex near Newton Abbot, with 21.

Aeshna cyanea
Aeshna juncea
Agrion virgo
Anax imperator
Ceragrion tenellum (very rare in Devon)
Coenagrion puella
Cordulegaster boltonii
Enallagma cyathigerum
Ischnura elegans
Ischnura pumilio (very rare in Devon)

Lestes sponsa
Libellula depressa
Libellula quadrimaculata
Orthetrum coerulescens
Pyrrhosoma nymphula
Sympetrum sanguineum (very rare in Devon)
Sympetrum scoticum
Sympetrum striolatum

Lepidoptera

Speckled wood
Wall brown
Marbled white
Hedge brown
Meadow brown
Ringlet
Grayling
Small heath
Small pearl-bordered fritillary
Pearl-bordered fritillary
Silver-washed fritillary
Marsh fritillary
Heath fritillary
Red Admiral
Small tortoiseshell
Peacock

Comma
Holly blue
Small copper
Green hairstreak
Small blue
Common blue
Silver-studded blue
Large white
Small white
Green-veined white
Orange tip
Brimstone
Dingy skipper
Grizzled skipper
Small skipper
Large skipper

Reptiles

Adder; Grass snake; Slow worm; Common lizard

Amphibians

Common frog; Common toad; Palmate newt; Great crested newt

Birds

A wide variety, including breeding willow tits, occasional lesser whitethroats and redpolls.

APPENDIX 2

Useful Addresses

Avon Wildlife Trust
17, Whiteladies Road,
Bristol BS8 1PB

Botanical Society of the British Isles
The Hon General Secretary,
White Cottage,
Slinfold,
Horsham,
West Sussex RH13 7RG

Branch Line Society
The Secretary,
15, Springwood Hall Gardens,
Gledholt,
Huddersfield,
Yorks HD1 4HA

British Railways Board
Rail House,
Euston,
London NW1

Cheddar Valley Railway Walk Society
The Secretary,
Berrymead,
The Lynch,
Winscombe,
Avon.

Cornwall Naturalists' Trust
The Conservation Officer,
Dairy Cottage,
Trelissick,
Feock,
Truro,
Cornwall.

Cornwall Railway Society
The Secretary,
42, St Thomas Street,
Penryn,
Cornwall.

Countryside Commission
John Dower House,
Crescent Place,
Cheltenham,
Glos GL50 3RA

Cyclebag
35, King Street,
Bristol BS1 4DZ
(for information on cycleways along disused railways)

Devon Trust for Nature Conservation
The Conservation Officer,
75, Queen Street,
Exeter,
Devon.

Dorset Naturalists' Trust
39, Christchurch Road,
Bournemouth,
Dorset.

Libraries – Local Studies Sections
Avon – Central Library, Bristol.
Cornwall
Cornwall County Library
(Local Studies Secretary)
2–4 Clinton Road
Redruth TR15 2QE

Devon
West Country Studies Library
  c/o Central Library
  Castle Street
  Exeter EX4 3PQ
Dorset
Dorchester Reference Library
  Colliton Park
  Dorchester DT1 1XJ
Somerset
Local History Library
  The Castle
  Castle Green
  Taunton TA1 4AD

Lynton & Barnstaple Railway Association
The Secretary,
Lynton Railway Station,
Lynton,
North Devon.

Plymouth Railway Circle
The Secretary,
17, Birchfield Avenue,
Beacon Park,
Plymouth PL2 3LA

The Railway Magazine
The Editor,
Quadrant House,
The Quadrant,
Sutton,
Surrey SM1 5AS
(for photostat copies of articles –
state volume number)

Railway Ramblers
The Secretary,
11, Milverton Avenue,
Leicester LE4 0HY

Ramblers' Association
1/4, Crawford Mews,
York Street,
London W1H 1PT

Somerset & Dorset Railway Trust
The Membership Secretary,
35, Stamford Avenue,
Styvechale,
Coventry CV3 5BW

Somerset Trust for Nature Conservation
Fyne Court,
Broomfield,
Bridgwater,
Somerset TA5 2EQ

BIBLIOGRAPHY

Anthony, G. H., *The Hayle, West Cornwall and Helston Railways*, Oakwood Press (1968)

Appleton, Dr. J. H., *Disused Railways in the Countryside of England and Wales* (Report to the Countryside Commission) HMSO (1970)

Atthil, Robin, *Mendip – a new study* (ed.), David & Charles (1976)

—— *The Curious Past*, Wessex Press (1955)

—— *The Somerset & Dorset Railway*, David & Charles (new ed. 1980)

Catchpole, L. T., *The Lynton & Barnstaple Railway*, Oakwood Press (6th ed. 1972)

Clamp, Arthur L., *Let's explore old railways in Devon*, Westway Publications

Cockman, F. G., *Discovering Lost Railways*, Shire Publications (3rd Ed. 1980)

Farquharson-Coe, A., *Devon's Railways*, Viewing Devon series, James Pike Ltd. (1974)

John Grimshaw & Associates, and Cyclebag, Bristol, *A Study of Disused Railways in Avon and North Somerset*

Hall, R. M. S., *The Lee Moor Tramway*, Oakwood Press

Kendall, H. G., *The Plymouth & Dartmoor Railway*, Oakwood Press (1968)

Kidner, R. W., *The Railways of Purbeck*, Oakwood Press

Lovett Jones, Gareth, *Railway Walks*, Pierrot Publishing (1980)

The Railway Magazine, various articles

Madge, Robin, *Railways round Exmoor*, Exmoor Press (1975)

Maggs, Colin, *Railways to Exmouth*, Oakwood Press (1980)

—— *The Barnstaple & Ilfracombe Railway*, Oakwood Press (1978)

—— *The Seaton, Sidmouth and Lyme Regis Branches* (with P. Paye), Oakwood Press (1979)

—— *The Weston, Clevedon & Portishead Railway*, Oakwood Press

Peters, Ivo, *The Somerset & Dorset – An English Cross-Country Railway*, Oxford Publishing Co. (1974)

Prideaux, Brown and Ratcliffe, *History of the Lynton & Barnstaple Railway*, David & Charles (1980)

Sellick, R. J., *The Old Mineral Line*, Exmoor Press (1976)

Thomas, David St J., *A Regional History of the Railways of Great Britain – Vol. 1: The West Country*, David & Charles (5th ed. 1981)

Winscombe Parish Railway Walk Committee, *Cheddar Valley Railway Walk – A Proposal*

ACKNOWLEDGEMENTS

My grateful thanks are due to the following people for their help and encouragement:

Nigel Willis, who let me use his notes on the Callington branch and with his family aided and abetted me in many other ways; Robin Atthill, who showed me over the Oakhill Brewery branch and the Weston, Clevedon & Portishead Railway; Russell Pollinger and family, for welcoming a muddy stranger so kindly and for cuttings from local newspapers; Harry Lambert, ex-Oakhill Brewery driver, for his stories about the line; S. Behr of the Railway Ramblers and Bernard Mills, Secretary of the Plymouth Railway Circle, for detailed information on West Country lines; Geoff Snell, for up-to-date news of the Somerset & Dorset; Bill Pryor and family, for a welcome cup of tea in Lynton Station; Mr and Mrs Smallacombe, for the same in Ashbury Station; and Mr and Mrs Barattini and Mr and Mrs Richmond of the Mendip Society for showing me the route of the footpath they hope to see established along the Cheddar Valley line.

For their permission to quote from their work, I would like to thank Sir John Betjeman and Mr J. N. Slater (Editor of *The Railway Magazine*), also Mr Roche, who I have been unable to trace, for borrowing a verse from his poem about the Lan'son Goods.

I am also indebted to Caroline Steel of the Devon Trust for Nature Conservation, Karen Jefferies of the Nature Conservancy Council and Dr and Mrs Turk for their help with matters botanical; Mr C. Pettit, Assistant Reference Librarian (Local Studies), Dorset County Library; Mr O. Baker, East Devon Area Librarian; Mr G. T. Knight, Cornwall County Local Studies Librarian; Mr. D. Bromwich, Somerset Local History Librarian; Mr K. Brown, Somerset County Principal Planning Officer; and Mr A. T. Swindall, Dorset County Planning Officer.

I would also like to thank Richard Scott Simon and Vivien Green for all their encouragement; Hunter Davies, for introducing me to them; Nick Walford, for making silk purse prints out of sows' ear negatives; Cathy Donald and Brenda Cox for their typing double-act; my wife and children for making the whole thing possible; Nick Dent, the go-between; and a host of landlords and landladies, farmers and station-dwellers, dog-restrainers and lift-providers, railway enthusiasts and fellow ramblers whose friendly assistance helped me in many ways.